BOOKS BY PATRICIA O'BRIEN

The Woman Alone
Staying Together: Marriages That Work

Random House   New York

staying together

staying together

marriages that work

Patricia O'Brien

Random House   New York

Library of Congress Cataloging in Publication Data

O'Brien, Patricia.
  Staying together.

  Bibliography: p.
  1. Marriage—United States—Case studies.   2. Married people—United States—Interviews.   I. Title.
HQ536.026   301.42'7   76–53489
ISBN 0–394–49642–6

Manufactured in the United States of America
2 4 6 8 9 7 5 3
First Edition

For my spirited,
loving and essential children:
Marianna, Margaret,
Maureen and Monica Koval

acknowledgments

With all my thanks and affection to

Ellen Goodman, who shared many expensive phone bills exploring ideas;

Bill Cole, Dean of the Medill School of Journalism at Northwestern University, and to the many other people at Medill who offered their interest and support;

Michael Brewer, for his special assistance;

Charlotte Mayerson, my editor, a woman of warmth and consideration;

Roberta Pryor, my agent, for her active interest and solid advice;

and to Paul Nelson, for caring enough to get me moving when I needed a push and for encouraging me when I needed praise —mostly, for just caring.

contents

staying together

introduction

It is May 10, 1973. I walk down this street tonight, this street of home and marriage and family, and the warmth of the lighted windows angers me. I resent their promise, because this is the night that I know my marriage of fifteen years is over. They symbolize a cohesion and continuity I must now find elsewhere. But when I lived, married, behind similar windows, I knew the warmth could be false.

So as I walk and look and think, I take a peculiarly soured comfort in the thought that the people behind those windows have problems that might be worse than mine. They may even hate each other. Maybe they throw dishes and cry and stomp around and maybe they too will soon be, as I am, a divorce statistic. I conclude, in my needful, fuzzy-minded state, that soon all the world will be divorced, stagnating, or unhappily married.

And of course, I am mistaken.

It is June 30, 1975. An early summer evening in Chicago, and I am eating a plate of green noodles at Riccardo's

Restaurant on Rush Street. An assistant city editor from the *Sun-Times* walks in with the early edition of tomorrow's paper, and the big news is that Ann Landers, quite possibly the most famous columnist in the world, a woman who has symbolized stable values to millions of married men and women, is about to be divorced.

That announcement startles me. And it startles my friends around the bar. We talk about Ann, the symbol of American morality, and Eppie Lederer, the real person who has written for her readers a touching explanatory denouement to thirty-six years of what she calls "one of the world's best marriages that didn't make it to the finish line." But it is Ann as Symbol who shocks. I wonder what her readers will think. Will there be a rising, plaintive cry from all the husbands and wives who have brought her their problems of impotence, frigidity, Saturday-night drinking, I-am-the-Other-Woman-and-I-love-him, and I-am-the-Wronged-Wife-and-help-me-save-my-marriage? Will they say, "Ann Landers, you always come through. You're tough, you're practical, you make such heartening sense in a confusing world. Ann, say it isn't so. For if you can't make it, then who can?"

I think they will say these things.

And my wringing my hands over the crashing of one more symbol of marriage, this, too, is a mistake.

This is a book about marriage. More precisely, it is a book about men and women who are married because they want to be. It is a book about how people live within marriage, not solely "for the sake of the children" or because life offers nothing better at the moment, but because there is a special relationship they share that they value highly.

When W. H. Auden observed that "any marriage, happy, or unhappy, is infinitely more interesting and significant than any romance, however passionate," he was right. It holds true not only for the on-again, off-again marital saga of Elizabeth Taylor and Richard Burton, but for the outwardly dull and dreary union of a tax accountant and mother of three. But marriage is so complicated, so hard to understand that even the poets avoid writing about it. It's much easier to convey the short, intense bursts of joy and despair of romance.

For over a year now, I have been thinking about marriages. And I have found myself in the following conversation, oh, so many times:

"What will your book be about?"

"It's about marriage—marriages that work."

"Really? Have you found any?"

The response, I venture, is a one-liner that says a great deal about what we think of ourselves. I've heard it from single people and people caught in unhappy marriages. But I've also heard it from a housewife at a cocktail party whose smiling husband chuckled in appreciation. I've heard it from a skeptical stockbroker who, with his next breath, told me his marriage was great. And he saw no incongruity. I've heard it from neighbors at picnics and from television talk-show hosts; at conventions; from seat-mates on airplanes; from cousins and friends and priests and people in the next office. Everywhere.

It's clear that the institution of marriage today seems to be something best held at arm's length, like a dead cat turning aromatic. The litany of gloom goes like this: marriage is on the down slope; marriage is an impossible institution; marriage is not forever; marriage is the Great Disillusionment. Marriage is Hell and sex-twice-a-week and boring parties and fights in front of the kids on Sunday morning.

An increasing number of people feel this way. In 1975 more than a million couples were divorced, the highest number in the history of the country. And new marriages dropped to the lowest level since 1969. In Cook County, Illinois, the number of divorces filed in 1975 exceeded the number of marriages performed.

One reason for the drop in marriages is fear. Who wouldn't be afraid with the national statistics showing us that each year there is one divorce for every three new marriages? People discuss the latest divorce on the block as matter-of-factly as they discuss the latest outbreak of winter colds. They see marriages in terminal stages wherever they look, and often openly wonder when everything will fall apart for them. That kind of apprehension is easier to handle if one can thumb one's nose, crack a joke, and enjoy the meager comfort of the we're-all-in-the-same-boat camaraderie.

Clearly, not everyone should be married. Marriage is now only one of a number of life styles possible and acceptable in our society, and that's good. Fewer marriages may mean better marriages. Furthermore, many miserable marriages should probably be ended, and the fact that this breaking apart no longer brings down the wrath and censure of society on the heads of divorcing husbands and wives is also good. To be single for whatever reason has not only become more acceptable in the past few years, it has become fashionable and commercially profitable—whole industries have sprung up to meet the needs of the one-person household.

And yet, tap a Swinging Single on a lonely Sunday, and you'll hear some thoughts on what is missing: a feeling of continuity and a shared purpose. Expressing those needs often is accompanied by the fear that there *can't* be any continuity. So to marry today is almost to make a political statement. It is to fly in the face of all that is supposed to be liberated and independent; it is to choose a repressed existence rather than a free one. All this, in the wisdom of our current times, is against individuality and therefore suspect.

I disagree. Unfashionable though this statement may be, marriage has rewards and pleasures as well as pain and discipline to offer and it does not constitute the death of the individual. It is not a pathological institution. A volcano has not erupted in every living room. For although it is true that divorce is likely to claim 30 percent of all existing first marriages of people between the ages of thirty-five to forty-four, that still leaves 70 percent intact, and they aren't all miserable, nor are all the people in them resigned to lives that don't measure up to their original specifications.

In other words, not everybody is staying married because someone has to plow the north forty or because dinner parties with only one host are inconvenient.

Surely we can admit that someone is happy somewhere? Can we allow ourselves that?

Let's try it out and see how it sounds: someone is happy somewhere, and if that sounds like a line from an Eddie Fisher song, it's appropriate. The people in this book are those shaped and molded by the fifties, who stayed married through the sixties, with all that happened in that upsetting decade, and who are married now because *they want to be,* and not because they have no other choices. But what does this term "happiness" mean? What is a "happy" marriage?

A friend of mine, struggling with the question, came up with as good an indicator as I have found: "Use a ten-point scale of needs and expectations," he said. "If a man and a woman's expectations and needs are at the same level, they're happy. If their expectations both hit at around the eight or nine level, and their needs at six or seven, they suit each other. If their expectations are at two or three, that's okay too. It's when you've got one with a need level of two and the other with a need level of ten, that you've got trouble."

With this scale as the base, I submit the couples in this book are "happy." But that's the last time I use the word, for it means something different within each private relationship. These are not people living under glass. They face the same problems of anyone living at a time Margaret Mead describes as bewilderingly "charged with choice"; a time when freedom to choose any of a number of alternative life directions imposes incredible anxieties. Churning stomachs. Headaches. A bottle of Pepto-Bismol in every medicine cabinet.

The people who interest me the most are those of my

own generation, people roughly between the ages of thirty-five and forty-five. We were the children of the thirties and forties, grown to adulthood in the post–World War II glow of reunited families and the Valentine days of the fifties.

From my generation has come much of the current disillusionment with marriage, and a good proportion of the divorces. When we talk about it among ourselves (or to anyone else, for that matter) we remember how stupidly unprepared we were. We remember the nonsense of fifties romanticism, and many of us can't understand how our entire generation fell for it.

People were tired of being practical. During the forties, the men went to war and the women went to work, not in glamour jobs, but as machinists in aircraft factories, or as riveters, assemblers. When the war was over, these women passed on to their daughters their hunger for the frippery of strapless net formals and dancing the night away. The sell job was massive. We were pushovers. We wanted only to be beautiful, with Fire and Ice lips and lacquered hair that wouldn't budge in a strong gale. We wanted to be put on pedestals and courted. And so we were, because the men wanted that too. Who could resist Debbie and Eddie on celluloid and Daddy Ike and Mama Mamie in the White House? Crooners sang about love and marriage going together like a horse and carriage, and good girls knew it was a bad idea to go "all the way." A "nice" boy would want a "nice" girl, and their reward was to be a marriage that lasted forever, like a plastic rose.

A man who hesitated at the thought of marriage, who

wondered if indeed it was the best of all possible worlds, was not, as Philip Roth points out, considered very mature. He might in fact face the shame of being considered a homosexual. But usually he was branded as selfish because he could not "commit himself to a permanent relationship." Rarely, however, did a woman hesitate at the brink of marriage. It was very important to be married, very important to talk some young man into "committing himself to a permanent relationship" because a woman without a husband was vulnerable to both pity and scorn. So she deluded herself with an image of love that had more to do, as Roth puts it, with "the yearning to own and be owned" than with any true understanding of the person she intended to live with the rest of her life.

In this kind of atmosphere, marriage became a necessity. It became a duty. And because the demand was so uncompromising, so relentless, it became the antithesis of true romantic love. That was the big joke on everybody. A whole generation rushed into marriage without taking time to figure out what loving one person involved.

Marital roles came pre-packaged. The expectation was that the man would be forever the provider (which meant he was always supposed to be strong and reliable and heaven help the family if he ever broke down and cried), and the woman was the homemaker and not too good at balancing her checkbook (although she might have gotten straight A's in math through college). Children were a necessary part of the scenario, whether couples truly wanted them or not. All mothers were maternal; all fathers were proud.

Marital bargains, then, were based on programmed delusions of strength and dependency. As long as everyone bought it, it worked.

And then came the sixties.

We went from Ozzie and Harriet to Ted and Alice; perhaps more realistically, to George and Martha. The housewife who would have had four children in the fifties was holding the line at two, and taking care to gulp a tiny white pill with her orange juice every day. *Time* magazine proclaimed God was dead, and fewer families were putting on their Sunday best and going to church. Betty Friedan wrote *The Feminine Mystique,* and women everywhere, unhappy with their programmed lives, began thinking and talking about "the problem that has no name."

Increasingly there was a restlessness, a desire to push out the boundaries of individual experience. Men became dissatisfied with clock-regimented lives and women began realizing the Pill gave them not only freedom from having babies but freedom to have affairs. The people of the fifties wanted to be part of the sexual revolution of the sixties. They felt left out. Encounter groups gained respectability as the Human Potential Movement, and the message was "Please touch." Couples from Maine to Santa Barbara took off their clothes and exchanged bed partners, searching for what were now called "meaningful relationships."

This quickened pace of life, this rapidly changing environment brought a new kind of hunger into marriages, a sense of having missed out on a larger life. The constraints of marriage were all too obvious, and the disappointments all too real, for men and women who had struck their initial marital bargains in one kind of social environment were now trying to live with them in another.

By the seventies, marriage was supposed to be dead. Communal love, open marriage: these were the life styles of the future.

And so, many of the marriages of the fifties headed for the divorce courts. But not all of them.

Over the past two years, I have interviewed dozens of married couples and have selected six to profile for this book. Parts of their stories reflect or contrast parts of others, but they do not represent a statistical cross section of American marriages. They are middle-class, they all have children, they are white, their marriages were apparently working.

—*Jan and David Stein.* David, forty, is a successful television newscaster whose income has climbed rapidly in recent years to about $75,000. He and Jan, thirty-seven, and their two children live in a northern California city, where David's celebrity keeps an element of the fishbowl in their lives.

—*Dorine and Bert Brosky.* Bert, forty-four, has worked as a machinist most of his life, and is proud of the fact that he is now foreman over his own crew and bringing home $22,000 a year. He and Dorine, forty-two, have lived dutiful Catholic lives, producing five children, and have never quite had the feeling of being in control of what happens to them.

—*Diana and Phil Morris.* At thirty-nine, Phil is a moderately successful novelist, but he hungers for fame. Diana, thirty-seven, is a mothering person, a woman whose maternal and sexual instincts mix together intriguingly in her relationship with Phil. They live relatively isolated lives, deliberately shutting out most of the rest of the world.

—*Anna and Jim Lowell.* This was a marriage of two intense, far-reaching people which had many rich moments, many dry spells, and has, since the time of my interviews, ended with Jim's death. Jim, who was forty-two when he died, and Anna, forty-one, knew each other since childhood. Anna continued her education after marriage and became a political scientist, while Jim went into business. Eventually the tugs of their separate careers drew them into experimenting with a new life style: the commuting marriage.

—*Liz and Peter Arthur.* Peter, thirty-eight, travels all over the world on buying trips for his flourishing leather-goods business in New York City. He is a traditional doer, a go-getter, almost an updated version of Horatio Alger. Liz, thirty-seven, isn't interested in a career. She isn't interested in having her husband gone much of the time either, but she lives with it. Their lives at home revolve around their two children, and much of the energy of the marriage involves working out a living pattern that accommodates Peter's traveling.

—*Laurie and Bob Kincaid.* Bob, thirty-six, a doctor, is a quiet, conservative person married to a volatile woman who describes herself frankly as a "born flirt." This is a marriage of two people who have their share of painful memories. But their very different personalities have produced a blend that suits them both.

When I began the selection, some couples would approach me, either the husband or wife singly or together.

They would volunteer their own marriage for perusal. Sometimes, after long interviews, I concluded they were fooling themselves.

Could the people in this book have fooled me? Of course. But why bother? At one point or another, all of them have had marital problems, and some have considered divorce. The basic difference between them and couples who might be looking for a free therapist is that they strongly believe they have working marriages, and most of them hoped they might have something of value to offer to other people.

All of the interviewing was tape-recorded in the homes of the selected couples. I needed to get a sense of the rhythm of their lives: How did they act putting the kids to bed? Who was first to get up and get the salt at dinner time? Usually we just chatted for a while, no tape recorder on, with one or the other moving in and out of the room to fix drinks or turn off the lawn sprinkler. I tried to form impressions by watching first and asking myself questions: How did they feel about themselves? Was one more dominant than the other, and what was the other's response? Did they talk in tandem or as individuals?

I kept myself as much a neutral presence in the interviews as possible, and found the problem of being a third-party intruder less of a barrier than I had feared. I encouraged people to talk more with each other than with me, and was continually surprised at the extent of their revelations, which were often nonverbal. Sometimes I felt the tension of one partner resisting the other's description of their lives, and tried later to talk to this person alone.

The questions I asked every couple, basically, were these: What role has marriage played in your lives? Is it a central or only a partial force? How important is sex for you? Does it help hold you together or is it of only secondary importance? What about adultery? What were your romantic expectations at marriage, and how have those expectations changed? How do you manage the balance of power within your marriage? Is there a strong contractual theme? Is money a problem? How do you feel about your children, and how has parenthood affected your feelings for each other? Has the women's movement affected your roles in marriage? How do you feel about your work? When you change or face a crisis, who follows whom? And why?

Often I interviewed the husband and wife together and then separately, for if there is one absolute truth about marriage that I have seen, it is that in each unit there are two marriages: his and hers. Most couples dropped any form of "company behavior" quickly. (On one occasion, driving in a car with a husband and wife, I had the tape recorder on to finish an interview when they launched into an argument. I held up the microphone to remind them they were being recorded, but it made no difference. Finally, when they both demanded my opinion on who was right, I decided it was my interview time, not their fight time. I said it was time to change the subject. They did.)

I have no illusions that they exposed their inner souls, though sometimes they feared they were doing so. I have changed their names, occupations, sometimes the geography and some of the details of their lives to preserve their privacy. When appropriate, I incorporated illustrative details from the lives of other couples in similar situations. I learned a great deal, and I found I liked most of them. I might think they were making terrible mistakes raising their children or decide, Well, it's a working marriage, but it would drive *me* up a wall.

Yet, these are people concerned with the fascinating business of making a close relationship work, and that makes them thoughtful, if sometimes groping, human beings.

Anyone looking for reinforcement of the traditional vision of ideal marriage won't find it in this book. In other words, the reader will not find a reflection of what we *want* marriage to be. I have tried to look at these marriages as they exist in a continuum, not as frozen examples of unchanging relationships. In addition, there are many working marriages between people who lead unexamined lives. But the unexamined life, to borrow loosely from Socrates, offers nothing of value outside of itself. The best qualities of people, qualities such as curiosity or a sense of adventure, often operate *against* marriage. I am interested in how people with these qualities, with a sharp taste for life, manage to maintain working marriages.

Throughout the project, I realized that the responses to my questions touched not at all on the unique and private chemistry at the core of each relationship that truly keeps it together. How to get at that elusive quality? There seems to be no certain way. To write a book like this is to realize how unknowable human beings are, either separately or together. You can't walk into other people's lives and precisely measure the quality of human affection, nor can you fully distill the paradoxes.

What is "love"? What does it mean, to "need" someone? On the one hand, there is Lillian Hellman's explanation for her enduring relationship (which did not culminate in marriage) with Dashiell Hammett: "Without words, we knew that we had survived for the best of all reasons, the pleasure of each other."

The pleasure of each other. This I saw clearly. I saw it in the way a man would touch his wife's shoulder after an emotionally wrenching discussion of infidelity, and the way she would smile back.

There is another definition of love which is somehow gritty and sound: according to psychiatrist Harry Stack Sullivan, love is "that state reached when the satisfaction or the security of another person becomes as significant to one as is one's own satisfaction or security." In other words, when the balance is even. When respect and affection and caring for the other is equal to one's self-love—at least (let us acknowledge our humanness) on an undulating basis. This I saw too.

One thing more about these marriages. All of them have what I call a distancing factor. There's a particular kind of apartness that makes it possible for these men and women to hold on to each other without yanking reins; to allow each other a freedom of the spirit that most marriages simply do not tolerate.

One of the hardest lessons for men and women to learn is that marriage does not give automatic access; that no one can expect or hope for or demand to know or understand everything in another's brain and heart. Bertrand Russell, who thumped for marriage whenever he could, said it best: "If marriage is to achieve its possibilities, husbands and wives must learn to understand that whatever the law may say, in their private lives they must be free."

Ah yes, those possibilities. But with the courage to give freedom comes a sense of distant peril, for no one can guarantee his or her future emotions. Rhoda and Joe, pledging contemporary fidelity, assured each other and a national television audience they would stay together, for better, for worse, "as long as we both shall love." The marriage lasted two seasons.

A thirty-two-year-old x-ray technician, marrying for the first time, confessed later she kept her fingers crossed throughout the ceremony. "Just to add a little luck to all those promises," she said. There's a more cautious brand of romanticism abroad these days. More and more couples are entering into marriage contracts. Marvin Sussman, director of the Institute on Family and Bureaucratic Society at Case Western Reserve University, predicts contracts defining rights, duties, expectations, and mechanisms for mediation and arbitration will be the prevailing form of marriage law within a decade.

Where did we all get the idea that marriage was a solution and not a problem? Consider French social utopian Charles Fourier's theory that there are 810 distinct character types: 415 for men and 395 for women. Full "integrality of the soul," he says, may require two or even two thousand combinations of these character types per person. If he's right, the persistent expectation of finding One True Love and keeping it nicely static is sorry self-deception indeed.

I have met many people who insist that the best way to ruin a good relationship is with marriage, and it's easy to see why. Once a tie is binding, two things are immediately at war: commitment and freedom. Commitment without ownership, freedom with loving ties—marriage is a union of two individuals who will inevitably fight for and against both. At its most depressing, marriage becomes a relentless process of erosion with each partner chipping away at the essence of the other, each eventually killing off what drew him to that person in the first place.

All that said, I believe in marriage. I think it's trendy to dismiss the institution as a beached whale in the throes of death. Author Michael Novak may frighten more than encourage with his call for a return to the "disciplines and terrors" of marriage (Catholics will understand the stern choice of words), but his message that marriage is one of our best bets for leading balanced lives is valid. It isn't just a matter of exchanging an isolated if frantic singles life for a secure niche in the suburbs; it's the opportunity to really plumb what it means to love and be committed to one person. Just one. A psychiatrist, depressed after thirty years of marriage counseling, said to me, "Why don't people slow down and take time to learn about and understand this single relationship?"

I don't think we're any better off for trying to protect ourselves by assuming that love relationships can never be more than fleeting pleasures of life. That doesn't mean, I want to emphasize, that we all *need* marriage. I may never remarry, and the prospect causes me no sharp alarm. (In a specific sense, I could change my mind any day, which is part of the pleasure of the unknown.) But singleness has its own challenges and pleasures. To learn to rely on one's self can be a major and delicious achievement—particularly for women who, in our culture, are still programmed to be married and helpless, instead of finding their own strength first, and then choosing to be either single or married.

I don't for a moment think that the men and women in

this book have found any definitive answers about making marriage work, and I want no "happily ever after" message conveyed. Some of these couples may be in the divorce courts by the time this book is published. But after all, these are not marriages that have *worked*. They are marriages that are *working,* and the future is unknowable, both for married people *and* for single people. For marriage, as we know in our hearts, is neither Heaven nor Hell, nor is it necessarily forever. But it does offer us the chance to reach across the lonely space and touch just one other human being, in hope of love, in rejection of loneliness. It can mean permanence, exclusivity, intimacy, security, continuity. It's a risk. It can be pain. But it's not boring. It's not dead. It may be as close to what living intimately with other people on this small planet is all about: loving, touching, hoping, caring. If it is not possible, let us all tip our hats to each other and jump into the sea.

In the end, really, it is something no one can describe very well. And so I like the observation of Charles Williams when asked about the nature of "the quiet affection" which is supposed to replace passion in marriage.

"Well, it certainly isn't quiet," he said, "and it isn't exactly affection. But the phrase will have to do."

the celebrity trip

Jan and David

David Stein isn't really a big-time celebrity. You wouldn't recognize him walking down the streets of New York, which he does like to do—but only once in a while. He's happiest back in his own West Coast hometown where eyes widen and heads swivel and teenagers stop and giggle and ask him for his autograph. He enjoys the attention. He likes the fact that he is instantly recognized each night on the six o'clock news, that the station has his picture smiling out of the newspapers and on billboards with increasing frequency. All that means David Stein has arrived. And like most men who have worked hard and scrabbled their way up in the capricious world of television, he looks over his shoulder quite a lot. It's not that the competition is getting too hot or too close. David has lots of mileage left out of his "image": he's young, handsome, scrappy, tough, earnest and sincere —and he helps pull good ratings. He's all of these things on camera. And he's some of these things, some of the time, at home.

Jan Stein is dark and slight and nervous, a woman of immense energy who worries over every problem like a dog worrying a bone. She is happiest in her own home, in her own kitchen, a place of burnished copper and stainless-steel pots and pans, a place of security, predictability, and comfort. She torments herself with her own ambivalences. She doesn't want to be famous; she doesn't want to walk down the street and have heads turn and be asked for her autograph. But then again, why should only David get that kind of stroking?

Jan discovered sex in high school and it became not only her secret pleasure, but her secret guilt. She enjoyed the necking, the petting, the coy tussles with boys who knew the best places to park in the abandoned oil fields near her home.

She lived in fear of being found out: by her parents; by her classmates; later, by her whispering sorority sisters who, she was convinced, would never do such a Terrible Thing even though it was so much fun. Which made her very bad, very loose, very unfit for the fifties.

Jan and David met in 1956. They fought openly and slept furtively with each other. They decided to get married in 1957 and they kept fighting and they kept sleeping together —and with other people. It was a very bad beginning.

This is a marriage that teeters—a perpetual balancing rock that may crash into a dark and stormy sea at any moment. It is a marriage that is mostly Sturm relating to Drang; beset on one side by the husband's celebrity and on the other by the wife's search for her own confidence. It is, despite all this, a working marriage.

It is Saturday night, and Jan is alone with her potted

plants, her unbaked chicken casserole, and the television set. Her two children are at summer camp and she misses them. That bothers her because she feels she has become too domesticated. She misses the routine of Captain Crunch breakfasts and peanut-butter-and-jelly lunches and scoldings and mystery crashes in the upstairs playroom.

She turns on the TV and watches the attractive, authoritative newsman on the screen while he analyzes the latest political developments of the presidential campaign. She really doesn't give a damn because she wishes that attractive, authoritative newsman were where she thinks he belongs more often—sitting with her, at home.

Jan is morose, a not uncommon mood for her. She is thirty-seven years old and wondering a lot lately about what happens after the children are grown. They are only eleven and twelve now, but they are already restless, eyeing their own upcoming adolescence. And they say, "Oh, MOTH-er" a lot lately, too.

That's one of the reasons she went back to graduate school two years ago. It's also one of the reasons she wants to plan a career and not just settle for a job with a fancy, ambiguous "assistant to" title.

One evening two years ago, during a party parlor game, a friend asked her: "What would you do or be, Jan, if you could do anything you wanted with your life?"

Jan considers that idly curious question a turning point. "I gave one of those unconscious answers, I guess," she says. "I love the mystery of anthropology, so I told him I would like to be an anthropologist." She remembers pivoting in the center of the room, looking back into a mirror and seeing her own pleased, astonished face. "I thought, Who said that? The words just hung there in the air and I didn't really own them."

With David's encouragement, she plucked them out of the air, enrolled at the local university and started plugging through course work she found as comforting and predictable as her cooking. But now she is writing a dissertation, and she has a deadline, and she is frightened. "Right down to my *bones*," she says. She knows she fears any challenge that might have a question-mark ending; she wants to be dutiful and follow directions and have everything come out like a successful soufflé.

The news is over. Jan starts chopping vegetables for dinner. It is easy to see how passionately she loves her cooking. She doesn't work with a perfunctory assortment of equipment or foods. No tired salad of lettuce and tomatoes and a cucumber for her; she has artichokes and rutabaga and spinach and red peppers and green peppers, all tossed around opulent countertops inlaid with expensive Greek tiles.

Everything in the Stein home looks expensive; everything *is* expensive, and that, of course, is one of the plus factors of being married to a highly paid newsman whose face is known to everyone on the street. It means Jan and David live in one of those beautiful old homes of oak and high ceilings that are either torn down for urban renewal projects or become status symbols of the rich. It is lush with original glowing stained-glass windows brought West seventy years ago—thoroughly recaptured from the nineteenth century and thoroughly renovated, not cosmetically fixed up to fool the eyes of visitors.

Jan is very proud of this kitchen. "David is only a guest

here in the kitchen," she says, starting on the peppers. "This is my territory, and if he does things I don't want him to do in here, he's open to ridicule. I'm *merciless*. Just terrible sometimes. I'm trying to change that, but it's really hard for me to let go."

She stops, and stares for a moment at a spot somewhere up above the tiles. "It's my power base," she explains. "If I sit back and let him cook a meal, that means he can cook too, and I'm not the only one who can cook. On the other hand, it's really nice to *let* him cook a meal, so I'm torn. If I let him cook, I'd lose my power, so I complain a lot about his not helping me, but secretly I prevent him from helping me so I don't lose my power." She looks up from the cutting board with triumph, her eyes flashing with a partly wicked, partly self-amused light. "That's one that came to me recently."

The front door bangs open. It is David, home for a fast dinner before he goes back to the television station. He is not tall, and does indeed look boyish, perhaps a prerequisite for television. His hair is dark and his smile is very outgoing—he is warm and can verbalize his feelings easily.

He kisses Jan quickly, squeezes her hand in a quick, private way, then moves restlessly around the kitchen. "Set the table," orders Jan.

"See?" He shrugs. "I do my share. I help. I even do the dishes."

Jan smiles at him. "Love is a husband who runs the dishwasher every night," she says.

(It is David who wanted this interview. Upon hearing about this book, he said, "We've come through a lot, and it's good. Would you want to talk with us?" For two hours he and Jan discussed it, taking a careful pulse of their own marriage. They decided it was suitable, that it worked.)

David flicks on the TV set again, and Jan instantly looks irritated. "I've got a special on," he says. "Mental health."

"It's time to talk now," she rejoins. He turns the sound down, but leaves the set on. Jan brings dinner to the table without comment, and David draws his chair close to the table, trying to look as if he's gearing down. He tries not to appear abstracted; tries not to reveal that half, maybe three quarters of his mind might still be back at the station thinking about the ten o'clock broadcast; tries not to look as if he's wolfing down Jan's carefully prepared meals. He compensates with lavish praise: "Fantastic salad."

David is unashamedly ambitious, but he is thoughtful about his work. He knows television careers are fragile, ephemeral. He knows it's a mistake to believe the public image, which is so easily fashioned into something better than life. The short appear tall, the uncertain (with cue cards) appear confident, and the man with the right pitch, the right way of clipping his syllables, can project the most desired, most elusive quality of all for a TV newsman: authority.

David does it very well. He must constantly remind himself not to believe it all.

"I think, from the outside, to people who don't know us, I think David looks very flamboyant up front. There's stardom, and pictures plastered everywhere. He's onstage, really. There's a lot of performing," Jan says. "But behind it all, I do an awful lot of controlling. I'm really more of an authority person than he is."

To David, work is a narcotic. "God, a fantastic narcotic,"

he says. He enjoys the illusion of authority, but he thinks he has under control any wishful thinking about what that means. Asked what he wants to be doing in ten years, he confidently responds, "Running a skin-diving shop down at Big Sur." He fears growing old in television.

"When the end comes, I don't want people saying, 'Why didn't he quit when he was ahead?' You've got to force yourself to do something else. I don't want to go on believing in the truth of an image after the ratings go down."

When the show ends, David looks pleased. "Think it went okay?" he asks. Jan, who wasn't really watching, is honest. "I didn't see enough of it," she says.

He nods without comment.

"But I'll stop by at the studio tomorrow on my way to the library and watch the tape," she adds.

The conversation turns again to authority, the kind that says, "I will decide and you will live with it."

"Authority isn't really an issue in this house," David says.

Jan casts him a sharp glance. "David, we may not fight over it, but who assumes it? Or do we split it?" They stare briefly at each other.

David's head cocks back and there is a shade of defensiveness in his answer. "We certainly don't consciously split it," he says. "If I want something to go one way, and you don't have very strong feelings about it, then it goes that way, and vice versa."

She nods. Encouraged, he continues, "There sure as hell is no boss around. I don't wear the pants, nor do you. If you want the kids to do something, and I don't feel very strongly about it, that's the way it's done. When did this business of authority come up?"

(I explain that I am interested in who has what authority in making decisions—not who is the most powerful. Few couples are comfortable with straight-out discussions of power. "That's because," one wife told me privately and wisely, "the balance is fragile and often shifting. If we emphasize power, we become antagonists; if we emphasize understanding, we are still partners.")

David relents; the word is defused. "I think Jan makes more decisions than I do," he admits. "We rarely clash, because we each know what the other does best. Except when one of us is driving and the other figures we're going in the wrong direction."

"Oh boy, is that a tense thing," says Jan. "I tell you about directions and you get furious. You say, 'Goddammit, I never should have listened to you.' "

"Listen, you never know where we're going unless you've got a flock of maps," retorts David.

"You're making me very angry tonight."

The atmosphere is tense momentarily. But Jan and David decide to drop this particular who's-in-charge issue. Neither of them is interested in taking it anywhere. They are used to sudden, sharp verbal confrontations; they seem to develop them as a kind of exercise, an emotional calisthenic to keep their points of difference honed. In a curious way, it seems to be their pattern of behavior to guard against taking each other for granted.

It's late at night, when the children are in bed, after David drags home for the final time from the station, that they talk about the serious things. And often David's work is the first topic.

"His hours are shitty," complains Jan. She will often go to bed at ten, deliberately not watching the last newscast. She will lie there and count the floral repeats on the wallpaper while she waits, and mull over a familiar feeling of being left out, temporarily, but routinely shunted off. It's like a toothache, the kind one's tongue repeatedly returns to explore—more of a fascination with the presence of pain than a sharp experiencing.

And after weeks, months, years of this, she realizes now she is jealous.

In the early fifties, Jan had a favorite daydream, built from a hodgepodge of fairy tales, from memories of books filled with illustrations of tall castles and handsome kings: she was a princess in velvet and ermine and on her head she wore a crown that glowed in the daytime sun and sparkled under the evening moon. When she walked into the ballroom, all heads would turn, all eyes would stare with admiration. It is the dream of women who hunger for attention in a particular, look-at-me way. It is the dream, in its male or female variations, that finally, with rueful resignation, gets tucked away by most of us.

Jan fiddles with her half-filled coffee cup. "It would be fabulous to get the kind of attention that David gets," she says. "Everybody knows him. Women fall in love with him. People are always coming up and asking for his autograph. I don't want *exactly* the same thing. . . , but I'd like to get attention for what I do."

The attention comes—vicariously—usually in restaurants. Sometimes Jan likes it and sometimes she doesn't.

"People feel free to interrupt our conversation, even sit

down and start talking to David," she says. "Most of the time—well, some of the time—it's nice. Sometimes our friends get irritated with the interruptions."

"That's hard on me, too," says David thoughtfully.

Jan flashes him a partly amused, partly you-don't-understand look, but her answer acknowledges his point. "It influences our friendships, but I don't think it's a big problem. Sometimes the kids and I tease him about being David Stein, Super TV Star, so as to keep him down a peg or two."

"Sure, I like the attention," says David. "I'm not too inhibited about things, but I forget that people are watching me in public places. If I sometimes play my little celebrity game to attract attention, Jan gets embarrassed. Now we have a signal." He laughs. "When she hits me in the leg, I cool it."

Usually they prefer to have friends over because of the stop-and-go quality to their socializing. David goes to work in the morning to prepare his newscasts, stays through the six o'clock news, comes home between seven-thirty and nine-thirty, and then goes back to the station until eleven, six days a week. Jan's complaints about being left at dinner parties alone are less frequent now; when she is in her own home, she doesn't get the same jilted feeling. And David has worked out a smooth routine for "ducking out" for a little while, then coming back to the party. "It works pretty well," Jan says.

Time together, as a couple, as a family, is precious. When the children are home, the day starts early. "We're up long before seven-thirty," says David. "The children come into our room and pile up on the bed and we talk. Then I go downstairs and make breakfast while Jan is getting dressed

30

—hey!" He looks at Jan. "You're giving that look, like what I'm saying isn't what goes on."

"Yeah, it is. But it sounds smoother than the way it really works." She laughs. "I'm thinking about the toilet-paper nonsense."

He groans. "Oh, Christ."

"We fight about who does what all the time," Jan says. "David is really fantastic in helping me, and we share a lot of the responsibility around the house. But every once in a while, I get the feeling he's just a visitor around here. In fact, the person who really thinks it all out and makes all the rules and hands out the assignments is still me, and that's not equitable at all. So I get angry. Do you know David hasn't changed a roll of toilet paper without being asked the whole time we have lived together? I mean, he would use a *towel*. My feeling is, David would do anything rather than change a toilet-paper roll."

"That's not true," protests David.

"My point is, if the toilet roll is empty, the person who is there when it is empty should fill it," snaps Jan.

"Look, I don't have the time to think of those things. It's like the light bulbs. You're the one who wants the light bulbs changed, and what you want is for me to want the light bulbs changed the way you want them!" David delivers this with great vigor.

Jan stares hard, retreats. "I'm more compulsive in many ways," she says. "And when I'm feeling a little bitchy, I try to foist things off on David. It's really my own fault."

David looks gratified, but Jan is still thinking.

"Remember when I had to take that driving rap for you?" she says suddenly.

"We were driving home one night at two in the morning, and I made an illegal turn," he says. "I can't remember why I did it, but a cop pulled up in back and started flashing his light. I didn't have my driver's license with me."

"David, it had *expired."*

"Now, wait a minute. I was one of those unfortunate few who got picked to be retested, which meant I had to go out for a test, and that's a pain in the ass. I was driving on an expired license, but I've got a good driving record. Anyhow, the cop stopped us and I figured, Oh, my God, driving on an expired license—they're going to haul me into jail. So I said to Jan, 'Quick, give me your license.' So she did. You didn't even hesitate."

"Yes, I did. But I panicked. I thought, What do I do? and then I handed it over to you. God knows why." Jan's dark brows pull together and her mouth is tight.

David sits up straight. "So I gave her license to the cop, and he wrote out a ticket. It was in her name, of course, so she had to go to court." He waits.

"That meant I had to take the rap for him on a moving violation. And I was furious with him for making a wrong turn. The one thing I've always gotten furious about, is I let myself be put in a position where I'm taking the blame for him in a very bad situation."

"Look, the only skin off your back was an uncomfortable trip to traffic court, which in many ways is an interesting trip."

She looks at him with instant scorn. "But one you would never deign to take. David, you're always getting out of little, everyday things that other people have to do, because of your job. You get tickets fixed. The rest of us have to go to traffic court."

"If I had time—"

"I know. You're too important a guy."

"No, I just don't have time. I have a very unusual job."

"Well, you made that for yourself."

"Look, I could quit doing the evening news and spend two hours in traffic court and probably have a heart attack! That's not your problem, of course."

Jan relents a little. "Nobody likes to spend two hours in traffic court. There are a lot of people who find it difficult to take time off—doctors or teachers—not even including myself as an example! My whole position, David, is you wiggle out of things that other people have to do, and that time, I felt used by you and I hated it. I really hated it. It made me feel like two cents."

"If the situation had been reversed, I'd have done the same for you," says David.

"I'm not sure you would have," she responds slowly.

Jan and David met in a warming hut on a crowded ski run in Colorado. David knew immediately he liked this woman with the dark eyes, the funny, quick wit; Jan saw him as pleasant, somebody to see once in a while, but certainly not her "dream man."

But the typical "dream man" of the fifties never materialized anyway. David was persistent. He began queuing up at the Greyhound ticket counter on weekends, lugging his books along to study on the long trips to the tiny women's college in Vermont where Jan was going to school.

They would take long walks through the woods, and it was so romantic, Jan was embarrassed. What she liked most about David was his forthright manner, his practical, matter-of-fact way. She felt uncomfortable with mushiness.

She looks at David across the table. "You were not my really ideal romantic character, but I loved you."

"I gave you my honor achievement pin," says David.

Jan laughs. "The other girls had fraternity pins, so I had to come up with *something.*"

"Think of the romantic things I bought," protests David. "Like the little dog at the zoo. Remember? We bought it at the pet shop in the zoo?"

"We were too inhibited in the fifties to live together, so we bought a dog together," says Jan.

She resents that now. She resents all the guilt about sex. "I didn't do anything more then than what would be considered normal for a girl now," she says. "It wasn't possible. My family, my girl friends—they were all very shocked anyway by my freedom. I didn't feel I could trust anybody."

David understood. He also understood they couldn't keep flirting with the conventions, and he figured they might as well get married. It wasn't a carefully thought out decision. It was partly capricious, partly desperation for a bed to call their own.

"One thing we can never say, if our marriage goes down the drain," says David. "And that is, 'Where did it go wrong?' It started out wrong, and it got better." He shrugs, and throws off a what-the-hell line. "The best thing to do is be dumb and immature, jump into it, and if it develops, that's fine."

34

"We were lucky, David," Jan says quietly. "It started out very strange and very ignorant, and it developed into something very good."

"If you wanted to get married, it was fine with me," David needles.

"We were stupid. Getting married shows how naïve we were."

"Why are you now saying that we were stupid?" David says.

"Okay, you're going to disagree with me. But if people are smart, they have some trepidation."

"If we had discussed it and knew what the hell we were doing, we might not have done it, because it didn't make sense. And that would have been a loss."

A short silence. "Right," says Jan. Something shared spans the table.

They made the usual promises of fidelity; they said they would have and hold and forsake all others, but their promises were immature. David felt trapped. He had what he now calls "a series of one-nighters" during the first rocky two years. "I was just grabbing a slice of life as often as I could," he says.

"We got married before you were ready to," says Jan.

"Maybe, but those weren't destructive," he argues. "What almost broke us up was when I really got involved, and there wasn't any sex involved. I was just reaching out—"

They look away from each other briefly.

It happened four years ago, long after the juvenile acting-out of early marriage was over, long after Jan and David knew they would stick together always, long after they made those private vows without words that are at the core of a good marriage, long after they had their two children.

It happened because of a crisis in David's career that frightened him, made him feel he was never going to make it in television. It happened, simply, because he was fired.

The road up hadn't been easy. David spent years running down stories for prominent columnists, building up an image as the young kid who could go out and get a story and make it zing, make the big guys look good. He found he was adept at making himself look good, too. People remembered the earnest, hard-working legman who popped up all over town. And when he got up his nerve to take a crack at television, he was well-received. He worked hard. He developed a reputation for being brash and tough and sometimes he believed it a little too much, and put a few top-brass teeth on edge. At the network, he complained about things he didn't like. The public liked him, but he pushed against the station's conservative policies once too often.

And so he was fired. The shock was profound, but it was a plunge down that suddenly went straight up, when the competing station, larger, with higher ratings, more money and more viewers, offered him an anchorman slot.

The only drawback was those long hours which were to set the pattern of David and Jan's lives from then on.

"The hours were awful," acknowledges David.

"I think you really loved it from the start anyway," says Jan. "You were nervous about telling me how much you liked it because you knew I'd get hysterical, so you eased yourself into it, and I got hysterical anyway."

"Jan was impossible," David says. "It was such a tremen-

36

dous opportunity and it was important to me for emotional as well as professional reasons." He smacks the table with his fist. "To be bounced out of that place and then come back as the star is pretty great. To be able to tell all those shmucks that kicked me around that now, when I would say 'Waltz,' they'd have to, if they ever wanted me back."

"What was hard for me was, I was cast as one of those shmucks," says Jan. "I was being kicked around, too. Here you were, the star who had risen, and everybody was loving you, and I felt completely left out."

There is a silence. "I think that if we stop to look at it, things changed for us then," says David.

"Up until that time I was your big supporter," she says quietly. "When you moved, all of a sudden the people hiring you were your big supporters. I fell into the role of downgrader, and I was angry and jealous. They were the ones saying, 'David, you're wonderful'; 'We're going to build advertising campaigns around you'; 'You're the kingpin around here.' And I was the one saying, 'It's shitty. It deprives me of you. We can't have any life together.'"

David stirs uncomfortably. "I know. You felt buffaloed."

Jan nods. "I clearly became the villain in your life, the noodge, the person who was always on your neck."

David leans over, touches her shoulder. They tell what happened; one talking first, then the other picking up the story. There is a peculiar gentleness to the procedure, as if each is helping the other.

David had thrown himself into the new job, determined to prove himself not just a survivor, but the biggest winner in town. He worked at the station twelve hours a day, feeding fully on both the pace and the praise. He avoided recognizing Jan's feelings of displacement. She was frightened and showed it by pulling at him, doing anything to get his attention. David met a woman who did not feel threatened by his work, who in fact understood the strains and pressures involved and thought he was terrific. He describes the classic scenario with embarrassment, because it was so tiresomely corny.

"I fell in love with her because she really appreciated me," he says.

"And I was not appreciating you," answers Jan. "You were filling a gap."

David decided to "run away" (his description) for a weekend. He told Jan only that he needed to be by himself, to be alone to think.

"I told so many lies to get away."

"I really thought you were going away, just to think."

"Maybe I should have told you the truth."

"No, David. I think that might have been terrible."

When he came back, he confessed, with all the relief of the penitent sinner. For him, confession made the situation seem better, so he went on at some length about how he loved this woman, how he worried about Jan's dependence. How would she manage if they were, say, to get a divorce? But he didn't ask for a divorce. Future plans were left fuzzy.

Jan talked about the children. She cried and was angry, but, mainly, she was mortally afraid that David was going to leave her.

A week dragged by. One Sunday morning, Jan lifted the telephone receiver in the downstairs hall and heard her husband telling The Other Woman he was very concerned about Jan's welfare, that it was going to be tough breaking away from such a helpless, needful person.

Jan decided that was enough.

"It was like that flash of light that you read about but never really experience. I was most angry at myself. I really saw, for the first time, all the cloying, sort of childlike ways I had fallen into, acting the way I thought a woman had to act, and I hated myself."

She did not tell David about the overheard phone conversation. That night he initiated a discussion in a conciliatory tone, like a parent speaking to a child. Actually he felt rather proud of the fair and understanding way he was handling the situation.

"How dare you talk that way to me!" Jan shouted. "Where the hell do you get off saying these things? I'm not stupid, and I'm not weak!"

Jolted, David backed off. "Nothing got solved right away," he says, "but I began thinking about Jan differently, realistically. I shook some of the fantasy out of my head."

David's affair dragged on in an inconclusive way, but Jan began changing. She began reaching out to women friends for comfort, and for badly needed support. This was a very new thing, for women had always been her enemies. She learned early that a celebrity husband is considered easy prey.

"I figured most women were dying to get into bed with David, and my mother and sister thought the same thing. I never told them about this affair of David's. It would have been too upsetting. But I did tell them I was having this new and wonderful relationship with women, that I had two close friends who were really coming through for me, and that I was meeting other women who—well, their way of sharing themselves was wonderful." She laughs ruefully. "My mother said, 'Don't trust a woman. You're crazy if you do. As David's wife, you've got to mistrust them all.'"

She began to think about her marriage differently, to see it as a bargaining process in which she had negotiating power, not just a dependency role.

"It fascinates me how a man and a woman bargain in marriage," she says. "At one level, marriage is a power-structure of two egos, and maybe it shouldn't be that way. But you put two human beings into a life-long situation, well, you've got two human beings struggling for territory."

Jan fiddles abstractedly with a napkin. "We've worked hard at deciding how we stake out our territory," she says. "I'm not always comfortable with it."

David smiles at her, leans forward. "Gotta leave," he says matter-of-factly.

She looks quickly at the clock, and answers in kind, also with a smile, "Okay. See you soon."

Jan talks more about the changes that occurred, about the long, weary talks she and David had as, almost literally, they began renegotiating their marriage.

"I saw he was inevitably becoming more and more involved with his public image, and I would have to partly accept that. But I began to feel less devastated, less abandoned. I was finding substitutions, particularly my friendships with women."

She also found, temporarily, a substitute man.

He was quite a bit older, quiet and scholarly. He encouraged Jan to go back to school, to plan for a career, and to think of herself beyond the power base of her kitchen.

The affair was short-lived, ending without great pain or remorse.

"It was like having a daddy around, giving me lots of encouragement in a way my own father never had. I needed him at that time. I was terribly unhappy and I didn't know what I wanted to do, and I was terrified to commit myself to anything. I wasn't prepared to do anything. I had been a sociology major in college and that went nowhere."

Jan went back to school. At first it was mostly a transfer of dependencies from David to her lover to student-learning-at-the-foot-of-the-wise-professor role. "There were all kinds of mommies and daddies to take care of me and tell me what to do," she says with a wry smile.

When she completed her course work, she began teaching part time. For the first time she was standing at the front of a classroom, talking about what she knew and enjoyed. She was in command.

"It was the most incredible ego trip," she says. "Finally, I had a role comparable to David's. People write letters to David or stop him on the street. But they came in to have conferences with *me*."

It will be a long time before a teaching experience comes with status and tenure for Jan. The dissertation must be finished first, and it frightens her. She is both convinced she must complete it and convinced she won't. "I'm still trying to learn to do things because I want to," she says.

The sentence sounds forlorn, still a little childlike.

What does Jan value most in her marriage? What is in it that she couldn't replace?

She thinks a long time. "The friendship," she says slowly,

"the sameness, the continuity. It's coming home to someone I like and I love, knowing that we're there for each other. It's going to bed with the same person every night, knowing it's our bed, and we will be in it together. Everything else can be replaced."

Once again the door bangs open, and David is back. Jan perks up, exchanges a few jokes with her husband, the two of them flashing half-wary, half-amused glances at one another.

"How much of our lives is out on the table now?" David asks cheerfully. He doesn't pace the way he did before; he no longer seems restless.

What does he value most in his marriage? What, for him, cannot be replaced?

He scratches his head thoughtfully. "I suppose, over sixteen years, probably most of it could be replaced," he says. "I don't know the world out there, but I imagine there are other women with whom I could feel as comfortable as I do with Jan."

"I didn't answer the same way," says his wife. "I took the short-range view, like if we got divorced tomorrow, what couldn't be replaced?"

David answers again. "Familiarity, comfort, ease . . ."

A smile flickers at the corners of Jan's mouth. "I catch more positive connotations now," she teases.

"Oh, I think that's very positive," David says indignantly. "Every time I think that if I don't like it, I can get out, I start to think of the alternatives."

"Sure, I think sometimes I should get out and look around and make a new life for myself too," says Jan. "But it's not a comfortable idea. It suddenly occurs to me that there's nothing wrong with comfort." She pauses. "When I tried to answer that question, I was a little embarrassed that I liked the comfort, the coziness, the warmth of knowing it's you at home, the knowledge I don't have to put on. But you came up with the same stuff, so I guess it's what's important."

David begins to ruminate. "There's the house and the kids. I'm really kind of attached to this house, and I'm sure attached to those kids."

"That's part of my love," interrupts Jan, "watching you deal with the kids and knowing there's something really good going on among you. That's more of a loving thing to me than walking down the beach holding hands."

"How the hell would we divide everything up?" David says to Jan.

"Everybody who gets divorced has to worry about that," she responds.

David shakes his head. "They must really need to get divorced. They must really find it impossible to live with each other."

"It's been tough for us at times."

"It's never been impossible."

"Almost."

"But never impossible."

They touch hands and are silent.

It is long past midnight, and I am lying in bed thinking about the Steins, wondering how to convey the energy, the fierceness of this marriage. They have worn me out. Do I believe in them? Do they believe in each other? Do they care about each other?

What exists between them is not everybody's idea of a working marriage or, more to the point, it isn't what we might want one to be. But in all their arguments, in all their exchanges, there is an element of honesty that I've not seen in many a conventional, supposedly "happy" marriage. Jan is particularly adept at ego-snipping, but neither of them has become adept at saying one thing and meaning another. When they feel angry or hurt, they are not polite. They do not sit across from each other sporting tight little smiles like the brittle, biting dinner guests of Johan and Marianne in Bergman's *Scenes from a Marriage* (two wretched people in a wretched union, bent on saving self by destroying the other—politely, of course).

To say a couple is "communicating," as Carl Rogers points out, is a meaningless statement. They may scream at each other, lie, rationalize or ignore, all of which may, or may not be, communicating.

Just how meaningless this jargon word has become I realized one fall afternoon, strolling through Cambridge with an MIT scientist, a man of gentle wit, great warmth, and charm, in his mid-fifties now, married for close to thirty years to the same woman. "Early on, we decided, on no account should we be honest with each other," he said. "That is, in the sense that you sit down together and say, 'Now this is the way I really am.' That's insanity, because after you've said that's the way you really are, from that point on, you're sort of a cameo character out of a Grade C western. How do you step out of character after that? The idea is to be different things," he went on. "In essence, to play it sort of cool, and not really try to find out what the other person is like. That sort of curiosity is very restricting.

Very jailing to one's partner. It's a terrible thing. The notion of closeness has nothing to do with either possession or complete knowledge, you know."

What he was describing isn't a style that blends well with popular ideas of what communication is all about. To spend thirty years "playing it cool" sounds a little rough on the human psyche, and it's hard to imagine David and Jan following his advice for more than a week.

Still, the professor makes an important point about the dangers of relentless self-exposure. When two people sit down and talk things out at a point of crisis, they say things they normally wouldn't say. They figure it's time for honesty. So one says to the other, 'Back when you were working night and day, I had an affair.' Or, 'I hated you at the time your mother was visiting us.' Once these things are said, a barrier is broken, and they are easier to say again. Is holding back the truth a loss of communication? Not necessarily. It can be the wisest course for two people, on occasion, who have a long-term interest in making marriage work. There isn't a married couple (if they're honest) who hasn't done it, and it doesn't mean they aren't communicating.

Jan and David square off on many problems, but they have learned to be careful, too. Jan holds back her resentment that David's ego needs for public recognition get in the way of ego satisfaction in his relationship with her. His hungers reach outward, more than toward Jan. And when they are satisfied, she is jealous. Her own ego suffers.

It's a classic pattern for women married to men in public positions, be it in entertainment, news or politics, and managing the right balance is tough. Who wants to be invisible? Jan has had her share of autograph seekers in-terrupting a restaurant dinner, gushing over David, ignor-ing her. But she can't bang her fist on the table and tell them to go away, not when the attention pleases her husband.

The man reassured daily of his own public importance is a hard act for a home-and-hearth wife to follow. Myra MacPherson, author of *The Power Lovers,* points out that the political wife in particular gets caught in a double trap, for she appears "not only petty, but downright un-patriotic if she complains about a husband who is under the lofty illusion that he is saving the country." Yet the problem of getting private attention from public people is a universal in these marriages. Rod Laver's wife, Mary, told writer Jeanne Parr how her husband and her doctor both sat with their eyes glued to a television set watching the tennis matches while she was in the final stages of labor, actually turning to her at one point asking coolly if she could hold out for one more set. "You want to know what it's like to be married to a tennis champion? *That's* what it's like," she said.

And so it goes for Jan Stein, though I can't imagine her sporting a Pat Nixon smile through public travail. She doesn't like autograph seekers in public any more than she would like them popping up in her own kitchen, but she's got to live with it as long as she's married to David or as long as he lasts in television.

So how does one lead a private life with a public person? Bethine Church, wife of Senator Frank Church of Idaho (according to MacPherson, one of the Washington political rarities, a happily married couple), dealt with that question during a long afternoon interview. "I'm as involved as I can be with his life," she said, "I always travel with Frank, listen to his debates, and argue with him about his votes. And I've learned you have to build a private moat around your marriage when it's semi-public. You can't stop people from monopolizing your husband, but you can do things like go to as few parties as possible. Hold it all at arm's length, and hang in there, close to him."

Bethine Church's big advantage, of course, is that, being born and bred to enjoy politics herself, she had an early focus on herself and knew what she wanted. Her marriage is an extension of her early life as the daughter of a politician. That's an advantage most women married to public men don't have—they married the guy when he was still playing summer stock and moving furniture, or running the local school board. Stardom, be it in Hollywood or Washington, hits them between the eyes. They get shuffled off to starboard.

Jan doesn't have much trouble keeping David's attention, not with her volatile nature. And he gets passing marks for his concerns with their domestic life. But Jan's outside accomplishments cannot get the same public attention as David's. The very fact that David is routinely looking at the family from the television screen while they're eating dinner makes this a no-win game. And there's no way her own work will get David's interested attention, either, for struggling through a bone-dry thesis on anthropology just isn't an act he pulls off very well.

Part of the problem is the restlessness of a man wrapped

up in the fast pace of television. It's a life built around in-stant interests and passions which go into the wastebasket with each day's discarded wire copy. (I recall an acquaint-ance of mine, a national talk-show celebrity, who had an attention span of precisely one hour, which was fortunate, given the 60-minute length of his show. Working in the world of television often does have a negative impact on an individual's powers of concentration. Which is just a nice sort of bloodless, calm way of saying Jan has shed many tears trying to get more of that concentration coming in her direction than David has managed to deliver.

Jan's answer so far is to work harder at patting herself on the back, knowing it wouldn't be enough anyway for David to respect her ego. She needs to respect her own. I'm not at all sure that she wouldn't love to be just as publicly acclaimed, just as famous as her husband. She is basically competitive and ambivalent about it, at a time when it is tantalizingly possible, when a woman can compete. She might be happier and more secure if she hung on less desperately to her kitchen domain, and tried her luck more forthrightly in the "outside" world.

Jan actually is a woman straddling two definitions of self. She is controlled under the surface in a traditional, female manner; at the same time, she thinks she wants power re-negotiated. She wants David to do the dishes and button up the kids' overshoes more often, but if he does too many things too well at home, then what is she? David doesn't see it as a power issue. He sees helping at home as a gallant way of accommodating his wife, not as a move toward eras-ing the strict boundary lines separating their roles.

A recent Cornell University study of two-career marriages showed that husbands averaged eleven hours a week helping around the house, while their wives put in from twenty-one to fifty-six hours in the same period of time. "I've dropped the issue," said a forty-two-year-old woman who manages her own public relations firm. She spoke at the end of a twelve-hour workday, her feet up on the coffee table, shoes off, expression frazzled. Her eyes wandered past the dust on the living-room piano and the wilting philodendron by the unwashed bay window. "My husband helps me more if he feels he can do it when he wants to. There's no use telling a man he's *got* to do the dishes. He wants to feel he's doing a favor."

Given the fact that Jan's role outside the home isn't nearly as consuming or as focused as this woman's, it's clear why David likes to see his home duties stemming from generosity and not duty. As long as David and Jan play tag with the words they use to describe their home arrangements, things work. I don't really think Jan actually wants to give up one iota of power. She considers the sharing of home chores as a way of making what she does seem more significant. If David's doing those dishes too, being a housewife isn't so meaningless. Yet his general attitude of benign tolerance grates deep. She perceives it as condescension. Renegotiating is a confusing business in this marriage, for the focus on what comes out of the process isn't clear. Still, it's the battling honesty with which David and Jan tackle their problems that makes the difference.

This brings up the painful crisis of David's affair, an event they handled with their usual mixture of tears and anger. Like every other couple in this book, infidelity came to the Steins as a result of crisis, and they dealt with it on that basis. Jan and David married with an incompatible mix of sexual and emotional needs. Jan was a childhood romantic dreamer, but by the time courtship came, she was already more practical, certainly more so than David. She speaks of his "mushiness" with remembered embarrassment, and it is clearly David who felt romantically thwarted after marriage. Sometimes the two of them would hike out across a deserted beach, find a shielding rock, take their clothes off, and make love. For David, this was exciting. For Jan, it was a devil of a problem in the sand. It wasn't a lack of sexual responsiveness, but Jan prefers order: locked doors, lights out—her concession perhaps to all the early parental and peer disapproval. Both of them insist that David's early unfaithfulness wasn't a problem; they gloss over the one-nighters with an impatience that relegates them to the level of importance of, maybe, a dieter's midnight raid on the refrigerator. But they see the long-term love affair as a different thing, as much more than an exercise in sexual exploration. David needed reassurance that he was terrific, that he was lovable, that he was desirable. Jan needed reassurance that she was intelligent, that she was needed, that she was lovable. They were two leaning towers ready to crash.

I've watched others hit the ground under similar circumstances. A landscape architect and his wife in Reno, Nevada, two people whose marriage had been filled with the small pleasures of their differences (he, quiet, lean, sparing in words; she, freckled, ebullient, always up), hit the same crisis. He began an affair with his secretary which he covered up for months, at a time when business was going poorly and his wife had gone back to college. At night she would cook dinner, put the children to bed, spread out her books on the kitchen table, and not speak a word until after the ten o'clock news. He would sit in front of the television set and simmer. Unsure of herself, she simmered too, waiting for him to admire her tenacity, her study habits—anything to reassure her that she was going to make it. By the time a neighbor began dropping elaborate hints about her husband's late hours at the office, the gulf between these two was unbridgeable. Ashamed, embarrassed ("The whole goddamned town knew!"), she demanded a divorce. Without ever figuring out what was actually wrong between them, they acted on the symbolic crisis rather than the real one.

Why do things go differently for Jan and David? Neither is constitutionally able to keep quiet about what's bothering them for very long, and they were realistic about their priorities. Their marriage was for saving, if possible. Jan's battling back strengthened her self-confidence. She began acknowledging her own fearful, babyish ways. Instead of dissolving when she found herself the object of pity by her husband and his lover, she took control of herself. David? If anything, his need for Jan is greater than hers is for him. She is an anchor he clings to, a reality amidst the fantasy world of public acclaim.

Neither of them took Jan's affair too seriously. They saw it for what it was: an effort to reach out for a parent, a mentor—someone to reassure and comfort.

Will these two stay faithful to each other? August Strindberg claims some people are born monogamous, while others are born polygamous, and that's that. (If so, it might save a good deal of grief if there were some test to determine one's natural category at birth.)

But Linda Wolfe, author of *Playing Around: Women and Extra-Marital Sex,* puts more emphasis on what she calls the "adultery-provoking marriage," which, as a process and not a contract etched in rock, is a changing thing. Certainly the Steins' marriage has gone through an "adultery-provoking" stage. My impression is that Jan is basically monogamous. Of David I'm not sure. It seems to me he will always have an eye out for other women.

They describe their own sexual relationship now as reasonably good, but I sensed a flattening out, brought on, I suspect, by the fact that David's hours demand routine times for love-making, and the right emotional time doesn't always fit the routine. Jan also has more problems coming to orgasm now than she did before. She attributes this to the tension of working on her dissertation.

Perhaps because of these restrictions, David and Jan play self-titillating sexual games. Not too long ago, after hours of smoking dope with convivial friends, the hostess suggested everybody troop upstairs and have sex—which they did, two by two, into each bedroom. It was a tame orgy, as orgies go. Each made love only with his or her spouse. Jan likes to tell that story. "It shows how really square we are," she said.

Perhaps more than for love, people marry and stay married for a sense of life. This will always be a high-intensity marriage, one where, as Merle Shain puts it, "Some decades will be better than others." Jan and David each bring energy to their union, an energy that has a life of its own. They never bore each other. They are never bored.

Marriage is dead without a connecting life force, something that provides a way to grow and change, and if that also means fear and uncertainty—well then . . .

As both Jan and David said, in different ways, consider the alternatives.

the traditionalists
Dorine and Bert

Pollsters love people like Dorine and Bert Brosky because they seem so comfortably predictable. They live confined and careful lives where everything takes place at its proper time: there is a time to go school, to find a job, to get married, to have a baby. They are the levelers, the ones who round out the mountaintops and fill in the valleys: they buy the color-television sets, they go to church on Sunday, they join the PTA and they play on the office softball team.

Dorine and Bert were married in 1956 after a two-year courtship. They have five children and a house too small to keep seven people from frequently getting on each other's nerves. But Bert's salary as foreman in a machinist shop in Detroit won't stretch any further. They live on a financial tightwire. Every week Dorine cashes Bert's check and carefully puts the money into envelopes marked "mortgage," "heat," "telephone." At the end of the month she takes the fattened envelopes downtown and pays their bills.

It is a workable system, but Dorine is restive because she

has come to realize how it symbolizes the way she and Bert carefully parcel out their lives. Everything is in its proper envelope. Anger. Dreams. And love.

"It would be nice to mix it all up a little," she says. Her voice is very soft, with a particular singsong, dutiful quality learned long ago from the nuns in the parochial school she attended. It isn't exactly defiant, as defiant statements go. Just containably wistful.

Is this, then, the same Dorine Brosky who sits at her dining-room table, pounds her fist on the table and says, "I want to assassinate the Pope"?

It is. Goodbye, pollsters.

Bert has his own problems these days. He is forty-four and life doesn't taste all that delicious to him either. His hair is thinning and his pale-gray eyes look anxious. He has a habit of watching his wife with something of a startled look. But I don't think he expects any surprises. He knows Dorine very well, and she knows him.

Every now and then, they tell each other to go to hell. They get tired of the routine of punching the time clock and working on their marriage.

"Be careful what time you come out," Dorine told me over the telephone. "The train runs through a pretty rough part of town." So I left before twilight on the long ride out to the suburb west of Detroit where the Broskys have lived for fifteen years. It is a neighborhood of brick and frame homes of no particular character, but it is neat and proud. Its inhabitants resent the fact that they must travel through a kind of urban no man's land to reach their homes. They don't want to watch their purses and warn their daughters and think of switchblades and guns. But as long as they can keep the moat between their neighborhood and that of the feared blacks, they are willing to put up with in-transit dangers.

Dorine and Bert meet me at the train station. They are solicitous and shy and not too sure about the tape recorder swinging from my shoulder.

"Do people tell you everything about themselves?" Dorine asks.

"God, no," I say.

They relax.

The Brosky home is old, set back from the street with about a fourteen-inch ribbon of city-green grass. Bert kicks at some toys as we go up the porch steps, nodding ruefully toward the porch interior. "In the past eight years I've finally managed to give it half a coat of white paint," he says.

Inside, the home has the same half-finished look. Rooms wander back and around, looking as if they were added or expanded at times of intense need and limited funds. The tiny backyard has disappeared beneath the presence of a huge marine-blue plastic pool. Only patches of soggy grass survive.

In the dining room, fiberglass draperies hang limply from the windows, but the room is warm and alive with pictures of children everywhere.

Dorine smiles as I study the pictures. "We're pretty child-centered," she says.

There are noises from the kitchen. Bert, who is bringing

in a strawberry shortcake dessert, barks once. As he comes into the dining room, he transfers a residual glare to Dorine.

"Not always," he says.

Dorine and Bert both grew up in Detroit. They attended the same Catholic grammar school, and met when Dorine was in the eighth grade. Dorine went on to a Catholic high school, while Bert was sent to public school. Catholicism was, by then, rooted deeply in them both.

"I don't think I was as influenced as Dorine was," says Bert. "I could take things or leave them, so to speak."

"Still, Bert, the Church has been probably the most important thing in our lives," Dorine says.

Bert nods. "Yeah, but it's not right that the Church makes it seem the whole purpose of marriage is having children. We met each other first, and there's got to be a period of time when the two people who get married are the ones who count."

Obviously, this is not a new subject. Clearly, Bert and Dorine share anger. It is in one envelope labeled "The Church."

Dorine, who was married in February of 1956, was a mother in February of 1957. That's the way things were. So they pulled the left-over wedding cake out of the freezer on that first anniversary and gave the baby a taste of the frosting. It seemed right and proper. Then.

"I was twenty-two at the time and I would have liked to share just one year with Bert. It would have been nice not to have had a baby so soon," says Dorine. "I think if I had it to do over again, I'd want to wait a year or two. Save a little bit of money. Kind of relax with our new life."

"It isn't that we didn't know each other," says Bert.

"Oh, I know. But marriage is different drom dating."

"Well, though, you can almost say we got running around out of our systems," ventures Bert.

"I still would rather not have been pregnant."

There is that slightly startled look on his face but it is followed with an agreeing nod.

"Dorine is much more independent now than she used to be," offers Bert.

Dorine laughs and pulls out, mentally, another envelope, one marked "Dreams."

"I wish I had gone to college," she says. "You know, I take evening courses all the time—things like brush-ups in shorthand and English—which is probably my way of soothing my regret that I didn't go."

"You liked that course on fixing cars, too," says Bert. He undoubtedly enjoys the fact that his wife can open the hood of an automobile and tell the difference between a spark plug and a water hose.

"I took a course in feminine psychology, too," says Dorine. "It was really good. It was about grooming, about attitudes, about women's roles, about self-respect and self-confidence and things like that. A woman came in to show us how properly to use makeup, and we had a film one time on how to relate to people, and another time a woman came in to show us what was correct in the latest fashions." Her voice is little-girl again. She is talking about new worlds for her, not old ones. It is strangely dated.

Dorine Brosky is more than just attractive. She has large brown eyes and a figure that has not expanded to fill her oversize kitchen aprons, and if her hair was not arranged in the Frozen Flip of the Sixties, she would look much younger than her forty-two years.

She is, I sense, a rebel in the world of plastic backyard pools. For one thing, she works outside the home.

"Just part time at a bank," says Dorine. "Which relieves the guilt a little. I guess other mothers feel the same way. What will the neighbors think? Will they say you're taking off and leaving your children, especially during the summer when all good women should be at home? But I like my work."

Bert folds his hands and looks at Dorine. "Sometimes I don't like it much," he says.

She nods. It is no revelation.

"I'm glad she has contact with the outside world," says Bert. "It gives her a chance to grow and meet other people —but sometimes . . ."

"I think the women's movement has opened the door for women to realize they aren't the sole child raisers in the home," says Dorine. "The husband has just as much responsibility. I mean, the home is still the basic place for women, but I don't feel it is the one hundred percent place."

"I help plenty," says Bert.

Dorine extends her hand across the table. "I know you do," she says.

"Most of my free time is spent in keeping this house going," says Bert. "I do outside things and Dorine takes care of washing the clothes and things like that. Occasionally she'll ask me to put in a load or something like that."

"Do you mind?" teases Dorine.

"Yeah. Sometimes."

"Well, you've got lots to do." She turns to me. "Bert had to take a test to be a foreman at his job. He was up against a lot of competition and he scored higher than anyone. I'm extremely proud of him." She speaks matter-of-factly. There isn't a hint of eyelash-batting.

Bert stirs and says, "Sometimes I wish my job wasn't so frustrating, though. Dealing with people can be a pain—so much pettiness and nit-picking. Sometimes I feel I'd rather be back with the tools and doing the job."

"The money is nice," says Dorine.

"I'm making about twenty-two thousand dollars now," says Bert. "That's better than anything we ever expected."

Dorine and Bert had modest expectations when they married. With the precision of mapmakers, they planned out the details of how they would live, and very little was left to chance.

"We saved for the wedding and bought our furniture in advance," says Bert. "We just took for granted that we were going to make it work. So we got involved in all these planning details figuring nothing was ever going to go wrong."

They smile ruefully at each other.

"We've had plenty of things go wrong," says Dorine.

The hardest part of the second year was trying not to get pregnant again. And Dorine, pushing back against her years of Catholic indoctrination, wanted to talk to a priest about using birth control.

"We just wanted to use rhythm," she says. "When the

reality of that first little baby came, I thought, I can't believe I'm supposed to go ahead and have another one."

Bert agreed to consult the parish priest. And after that brief visit with an indignantly idealistic cleric, he walked home through the snow, angry, his heart heavy.

"I didn't know how to tell Dorine at first," he says. "It wasn't a question of not wanting any more children. We just wanted to have a break so we could get back on our feet. So we could have the child to play with for a while."

Even now, nineteen years later, Bert is still pleading their case.

He walked in the door and put his arms around Dorine. "We can't do it, honey," he said. And she cried. It was so unfair.

"It was inhumane," she snaps.

The Broskys searched out another priest, an older man who had seen far more marital unhappiness pass through the doors of his church than the idealist fresh out of the seminary. He gave them permission to use rhythm. They were relieved. They felt freed. And they felt troubled.

"We began wondering about how our attitudes had been formed by the Church," explains Bert. "Is it right to go along with what they're teaching when you know it's wrong for you?"

"We panicked for a while," remembers Dorine.

Bert was able to shrug the fears away more easily than Dorine. He resented the humiliation of having to plead to use rhythm. And as time went on, it was clear that rhythm, as the old joke goes, was really just Vatican Roulette.

"We had a year's reprieve before I was pregnant the second time," says Dorine. "Then the third came along eleven months later. In two years our fourth son was born. Then a year later we had a daughter."

Somewhere off in the labyrinths of the Vatican, a struggle was beginning. As theologians argued over birth control, the Pope with great solemnity announced the formation of a papal commission to study birth control.

Catholic couples everywhere watched with interest. And hope.

"They ended up doing nothing," says Dorine with disgust. "We figured that was it. We decided it was most important to take care of the children we had."

For Bert, the decision was not hard. For Dorine, it was cataclysmic. It meant rejecting the never-before-questioned authority of her Church.

"I couldn't believe they would do nothing," she says, shaking her head. "There has to be a time when reality takes over. You have to raise children properly. You have to feed them and clothe them. You don't just hatch them."

For three months Dorine agonized. Should she use contraceptives? "Look," said Bert in exasperation, "if it's going to bother you this much, why don't we just forget it?"

Impossible.

"I wanted to assassinate the Pope," says Dorine. Her voice shakes with remembered anger. "Instead I finally got a diaphragm."

That ended the dilemma. The Brosky family, now permanently numbering seven, settled once again into the ordered routine that suited them best.

"But I guess we were different after that," Dorine says. "Don't you think so, Bert?"

He nods. "Yeah. We trusted our own opinions more."

Which helped when they began questioning the value of the Vietnam war.

There weren't too many Middle Americans criticizing and questioning the value of Vietnam back in 1967. They were sitting in their living rooms watching "long-haired hippies" demonstrate on their TV screens, and they didn't like it one bit. You just didn't question some things. The world still had to be Made Safe For Democracy.

One day Bert stared at the TV and then walked into the kitchen, where Dorine was preparing dinner. "I think the whole goddamn thing we're doing over there is wrong," he said flatly.

Bert is not easy with conceptual arguments. They are not his style, and he didn't find it easy to explain to his friends at the machine shop why he was suddenly talking like—well, like one of those long-haired hippies.

"Something just hit me," he says. "I guess it was just counting up all those deaths over there and figuring, if we couldn't resolve the important things in five years, what with the high costs and all, what were we doing there? Why did we have to try and change that country's ways to fit ours?"

The other men at the shop were angry. Bert wasn't sounding pro-American, they thought. Bert dug in.

"I told them, 'Wait a minute. Just because I don't believe the same way you do doesn't make me any less of an American.' And I said, 'Why don't you wake up and smell the bacon frying?' "

"I was proud of you," Dorine says. "I felt very patriotic back in the fifties and most of the sixties, but then somewhere inside of me, I began thinking, Are we all that great? Have I been too idealistic? Then, after Watergate"—she purses her lips disapprovingly—"I can't say I believe in our government as much as I used to."

Did Dorine and Bert feel like closet dissidents?

"We decided we were strong enough to think whatever we wanted to think," says Bert.

"That helped us figure we could be different from each other, too."

"We work together. We share a lot of things," says Bert. "But Dorine's right. We had to kind of let each other grow and go a separate way at times too."

"I had a weekend earlier this summer with several women up in Wisconsin," says Dorine. "It was a seminar-type thing, and I had to drive the whole distance by my-self—that many miles—which I'd never done before. Partly I wanted the chance to get together with women who had other views. It was something I thought I'd learn from. And also in my mind, I felt that it's good for Bert and me to be apart once in a while."

"Well, it wasn't exactly 'togetherness,' " amends Bert. "But we've gotten so busy, we spend too much time with other people. Too much running around."

Dorine and Bert are joiners, earnest, compulsive joiners. They belong to the PTA and two church groups and a choral group, and Bert heads a boy scout troop.

"Sometimes we're out to different things maybe four or five nights a week," says Bert.

Dorine responds with a shade of defensiveness. "We don't want to say 'no' to anything that involves the chil-dren," she explains. "We encourage the kids to be in the

band and scouts and things. The people running everything tell us okay, if you want your child involved, you
have to do your part, so we have to figure on going to all
the parent meetings."

"We want to be responsible about it," says Bert.

They both look earnest, and also tense.

"I've got feelings about children that I need to talk about
more," says Bert.

"Well, talk," answers Dorine.

"There's a band meeting for one child, and a cub scout
meeting for another one, and it's like we get meetinged to
death."

"We've got commitments."

"Yeah, to each other. When those kids come of age,
they're gone. That means we only have each other."

Dorine considers this for a moment. It is clearly not a
new topic, nor do they have polarized views. They both
feel overextended.

"The last time we had a weekend alone was about two
years ago, wasn't it?" asks Dorine.

Bert nods.

"It was really nice. We keep saying that once a year
we're going to treat ourselves to something special."

"And the once-a-year time comes, and we don't," replies Bert. "Last year the money wasn't there, and we kept
making excuses. This thing was coming up, and that thing
—all the different graduations with the kids. We become
more committed to other things than ourselves."

They look across the table at each other, and clearly they
see the years going by in each other's face.

"I guess we take our time together too much for granted,"

says Dorine. "If a meeting comes up and Bert and I have planned a movie together, I figure, Oh well, he won't mind if we hold off another day."

"Last night we managed to go out for a drink alone," offers Bert.

"And had a fight," says Dorine. "I think I had my expectations too high. As soon as Bert began to talk about home problems I felt we were wasting our evening. I let the mood pass, or it would have been a disaster."

"When you don't have a solution, how long do you keep agitating over it?" Bert sounds agitated.

"Well, it doesn't help when you walk away from it."

"All I wanted to do was bury the issue. We didn't need it."

Their tones have sharpened. Is this a bad time in their marriage? When has been the worst time?

"Funny you should ask," says Dorine. Her eyes fill with tears. "The worst time is right now."

There is a short and uncomfortable silence. Bert stares at his hands. "It's because of our eldest son," he says.

"You aren't authoritarian enough with him," says Dorine. "He's not a boy and he's not a man. It's a time when he needs a man to guide him."

Bert's expression does not change, but he is quick with his defense: "I try to talk with and reason with him. I've even tried force . . ."

Nothing much has worked with Mark, who is nineteen and out of high school. Mark loves his record albums and the stereo his parents bought him and spending long, lazy summer days up in his room listening to music, then eating the dinners Dorine prepares, then watching television and going to bed and sleeping until noon the next day.

Mark doesn't want to get a job. Mark, his parents believe, is rapidly turning into a drifter. And a sponger.

"He applied to one college and got turned down," says Bert. "Then he wouldn't try again. I tell him that he has to get a job to help pay for his expenses, but he couldn't care less about anything. I can't reach him and Dorine can't reach him, and I feel like saying to heck with him."

Bert's frustration fills the air. He cannot afford the continuing expense of a son who won't pull his own weight. But what bothers him and Dorine the most is that they feel perilously close to flipping their life-long child-oriented lives inside out, and sending their son packing.

"He needs to feel some responsibility for us," says Bert.

Dorine agrees, but her fists are clenching and re-clenching. "He needs a man to push him," she repeats. "I can't make Mark do what he should do as a son, but I think you could do more for him as a father."

"He just tunes me out," protests Bert. "And when he does that, I figure, Okay, I won't try. Sure it bothers me that I have no solution. I don't know how to come up with one. I feel stymied."

The solution both Bert and Dorine hope for is that their son will decide to go to college. They dream of that. They want it very much.

"We never had that chance," says Dorine.

"We talk a lot about it," says Bert. "But if he wants to go, he's still got to help."

Dorine goes to the kitchen for coffee and Bert leans back, the lines of tension relaxing in his face.

"Something you should know," he says awkwardly. "Just

because we're at a down point right now doesn't mean there isn't love. We don't share as much when we're in a bad time."

Dorine returns with the coffeepot and more shortcake.

"I think when you've been married a long time, it takes longer to get back up from the downs," Bert continues. "It used to be when we'd be at our highs we'd be there a long time, until a crisis came along. Then we'd hit bottom, but we'd pick ourselves up real soon."

Dorine pours his coffee and kisses him lightly on the head. "We share the good times and the bad times," she says. "That's the way we love."

"We're trying to talk more about this problem with Mark," says Bert.

How has love changed for them over the years, other than the loss of resilience?

"I'd rather say something about how it hasn't changed first," says Dorine. "I have a feeling for Bert that I have never had for anyone else. It matters to me how he feels about things. I can't say I've been the most dedicated and self-sacrificing wife, but I'd do more for him than for anyone else."

"I feel that way, too. But it's also doing things without expecting anything in return."

"Oh Bert, that doesn't work for very long."

He agrees, after a short moment of thought. "Yeah, after a while sometimes I feel I'm not getting anything back, so I do a little less, until things start coming my way again." He smiles with a sudden thought. "It's like a game. I figure This is my wife and I love her, and then something happens, and I think, Wait a minute. She's expecting this of me now. Then I think, Well, I'm not going to do it this time."

"You were much more giving when we were first married," says Dorine. "All those early years, you were great with the babies. Changing them, feeding them, giving them baths, even getting up for two o'clock feedings. I never felt I was in all of that alone." She pauses. "Then I realized about five years ago, I wasn't getting so much any more. I resented it. And that's when I understood I hadn't given as much as he had."

At that time Bert and Dorine began talking, at first timidly, with some of their married friends about the problems of getting along with one another. It wasn't easy, because they do not come from a tradition that allows for easy articulation of personal feelings, let alone sharing them with anyone else.

"By gosh, we found they had problems too," says Bert.

"We even talked—well, somewhat anyhow, about sex," says Dorine.

Sex? It's not much these days, they both admit.

"A lot of that is because of the tension over Mark," explains Bert.

Dorine nods and says, "It's affecting us, no doubt about it. There's—there's more abstinence than indulgence, I think."

Her choice of words strikes me as so—Catholic. Abstinence is a word that sounds much more virtuous than indulgence. Is the Church, then, still a third party in their bedroom?

Dorine stops to think. She is slightly flustered. "I guess

you mean, am I still hung up on my guilts over the whole issue of birth control. Well, I'm really not sure. I think I was a few years ago. Right now, we're just too busy. It's not that we like it that way, it's just something we've slipped into. For one thing, with all the meetings we go to, it's late and we're tired when we get home. We talk about what went on at the meeting, sometimes until after midnight. By that time, we're dead tired and eager to get to sleep." She adds, "We've just come to accept it."

"Yeah," he says. "That's the way it is."

In the short silence following, I'm the one who feels uncomfortable. At first I wonder why, and then I realize: it is because I'm waiting for one or the other to say the lack of sex is more than a minor problem. In other words, doesn't it matter?

Bert stirs; he has picked up the unasked question. "I don't like the feeling, and neither does Dorine. We talk about it, but we keep going back to the same patterns."

"Maybe we seem too placid about it," offers Dorine. "We weren't at first. I'd blame Bert, saying, 'Well, if you weren't so tired all the time,' and then he'd blame me, saying, 'If you didn't get so busy with a hundred and one things,' and then we figured out one evening we were putting an awful lot of effort into blaming each other."

"That was a jolt," Bert says. "It meant I should put a little more attention into blaming myself."

"Me, too." Dorine's eyes are wide and very serious.

I wonder briefly about my unspoken question, and feel slightly chastened. I realize now what I had been expecting was, yes, that one would blame the other.

"Marriage is tough," Bert blurts out.

"You can't *relax,*" Dorine blurts back.

They both take deep breaths to say more, but Bert, who leans forward, hands knotted together, speaks first. "We have to watch constantly for the little things that damage us and work hard on them," he says. "Then sometimes we find we're working too hard on things that are kind of minor, and getting uptight because we're ignoring the good things."

"The good things never come easy," says Dorine.

Again the Catholic perspective of "Watch out—if you're enjoying it, it isn't worthwhile; and if it's worthwhile, don't count on enjoying it."

Dorine is looking at me, and I feel she knows my thoughts. "But the good things come," she says firmly. "Sometimes when things are really bad, I think about divorce," she continues. "It doesn't enter my mind much, but sometimes I find it more understandable why couples do get divorced, although I don't think we've ever been in a spot where we couldn't mend our marriage. But we're not above the danger line. It can happen to anyone."

Bert nods. "No guarantees," he says. "I think about it sometimes. Usually it happens when I figure we're struggling over this problem with Mark and not getting anywhere."

One evening Bert and Dorine sat down together, setting themselves the task of taking inventory of their children, in much the same way one would take inventory of financial assets and liabilities.

"We talked about each one of them, figuring what we thought could be improved," says Dorine. She stares past Bert, through the dining-room window. "I'm not saying we want perfect children. I'm just saying we worry about ours, and I think somehow we're doing the wrong things."

"Our second boy is too much of a loner," offers Bert.

"He doesn't have any friends," says Dorine, her forehead puckering. "He's an intelligent boy and he loves music, but he'll play with his own ten-year-old brother rather than with other fourteen-year-old boys. To me, that's not right. He's not retarded. He's not backward, but we wonder if he's afraid of people."

Bert sighs. "Mark started like that too."

Again the tension, the unresolved problem of Mark.

"We wonder where we've gone wrong," says Dorine slowly, her voice troubled. "What did we do? Did we give Mark some kind of silent approval for being a loner when he was younger? Is that why he won't do anything now?"

Bert stirs angrily. "It's kids today," he says. "You tell them they've got to kick in some money for room and board, and they can't understand it. It's like they expect parents to take care of them for the rest of their lives."

Dorine glances at her husband. "I still think you give up too easily with Mark," she says. "But I can't make you do what you should do as a father, and I can't make him do what he should do as a son."

"Well, I'm not going to knock my brains out over it," retorts Bert.

"Bert, if you just wouldn't back away from problems . . ."

I change the subject to something less volatile: money.

"We've never fought over that," says Bert, with a flicker of a smile. "We'll never be rich, and it's getting harder than ever before to keep our heads above water."

"My job helps now," says Dorine.

"Heck, honey, that's just part-time."

"Well, it's two hundred dollars more than we had before, Bert."

"Yeah, but it all goes out," he says, "It's frustrating. We can't build up a little nest egg where we can depend on it. It's like, you know, you're beginning to get ahead and you start to save a little, and something comes up . . ." He shakes his head. "I don't know. Maybe it does affect our relationship."

"We started our system of putting the money into envelopes when we got married," says Dorine. "Bert always gets his check cashed and brings it home, so it's easy to sit down and start dividing it up into the envelopes. I liked doing it that way, because I always knew just how much I had set aside for insurance and everything, but now—I don't know why—I've lost interest." She sighs. "And if there's any time I should be concerned, it should be now. But I'm just going through the motions of this weekly ritual."

"You're not as concerned as I am," says Bert. "We keep taking money out of one envelope and putting it into another one, and it bothers me, because we keep robbing Peter to pay Paul. Like I said, we didn't used to have this problem."

"You're good about it, Bert," says Dorine. "I know I can't spend an awful lot of money on clothes or having my hair done every week." She turns to me. "He doesn't have a fit, though, if I get a dress. And I don't feel so restricted that I can't go out and buy a pair of shoes once in a while." She pauses. "I do like getting my hair done," she says wistfully.

"We're better off than we ever expected to be, that's for sure," he says. "We manage to take vacations with the kids in the summer. I can't look back at the last twenty years and say scrimping has made life miserable."

"I just wish we could catch up," says Dorine. "We keep saying, in another two years, the braces will be paid off, and in another two years, the roof will be paid off, and then we can start saving for ourselves."

"Someday, instead of going camping with the kids, we'll go first-class—stay at motels—it'll be great. We'll still be young."

Dorine's eyes dance. "Oh, Bert, just think. We could go to the East Coast, and see Vermont and Maine."

"Maybe even the West Coast—maybe up into Oregon . . ."

Dorine and Bert are, together, looking into the envelope marked "Dreams." They are glowing.

"I can't imagine seeing any of those places without you," Bert says. He looks at me a trifle diffidently. "We do share a lot, you know."

It seems a good time to ask the question: What, then, is irreplaceable in this marriage?

There is a silence. Both seem a little stumped.

"I've got to say it's a feeling of concern," says Dorine slowly. "A real concern for each other. Bert is the most special person in my life, and when things aren't going right for us, we both know it and we both care."

Bert thinks a while longer. "I guess it's sharing," he says finally. "I can talk with the men at the shop about money and the way kids are these days, but I can't talk about any-thing—well, anything intimate. Dorine's the only one I want to share anything like that with." He pauses again. "One of these days all the kids will be gone. That's okay. And that's why I don't put them first in our marriage. When it comes right down to it, we only have each other."

Dorine looks at her husband almost shyly. "I wonder sometimes about what it would be like to be with another man," she says. "I mean, not seriously, but a man will walk by at a party or something and I'll think about it."

"Well, sure. Me, too," says Bert.

"Bet you wouldn't," answers Dorine calmly.

Bert shakes his head.

Dorine turns to me. "I just sort of have that faith," she explains. "Bert wouldn't feel good about himself, I think. He's a man who likes his self-respect."

"You, too," he says.

I flick off the tape recorder, and Dorine looks at it and says sheepishly, "That thing made me so nervous at first. I know it's confidential, and we'll be anonymous, but I've just never done anything like this before."

Two of the children, realizing the important discussion with the strange lady is now over, come bursting into the room, demanding their mother's attention. But she is still thinking, and she wants to tell me something.

"I was worried this morning," she confides, grabbing one child gently at the nape of his neck. "I didn't see how I could talk about the important things to you, but the more we talked, the more I thought, Why not? Why not tell her the things that matter?" She turns to her husband, who is scolding the second child for knocking over a glass. "Do you think we did, Bert?"

"If we're hiding anything, I don't know what it is."

I hope Dorine and Bert get to Maine and Vermont and Oregon and anywhere else they want to go; I hope they won't be too cautious, too prudent with their money. I think they have the capacity to enjoy, and to enjoy together. They are struggling hard to be good people against two major obstacles, the authority of the Church and the fact that they are parents. They exude guilt. And for that guilt, they exact a high price by putting limits on what they allow themselves to enjoy, be it sex with each other or spending money on anything not essential that brings them pleasure.

In their Catholic working-class world, the enjoyment of sex without producing children is still a guilty enjoyment, compounded for them by the simple fact that they didn't want all these children they have. They are just on the edges of acknowledging that openly. They've developed a life that on the surface revolves around the children, but though it is dutifully lived, it is not deeply felt. Four to five nights a week at church and school and scout activities may be superficially in the interests of the children. But it's really a way of fleeing the kids.

To be a parent isn't easy; to be a Catholic parent who didn't choose the role is harder. When Rev. Andrew Greeley (a sociologist and the Church's Bad Boy) recently did a study of what happened to Catholic couples' attitudes after Pope Paul VI's refusal in 1968 to allow contraception, he found a direct correlation with a precipitous decline in overall church attendance. Church authorities (those who suspected it all along) were noncommittal. Church authorities (those who dislike Greeley and/or sociologists) denied it. But few Catholics I know were at all surprised. ("Hey," said an old friend gleefully, "do you think Rome might finally wake up?")

It can seem almost amusing now, but it certainly wasn't a joke for Catholics in the mid-sixties. At that time, as a faculty wife at the University of Notre Dame, I knew many couples who finally decided they had had enough, and quietly began to use contraceptives. One of my more vivid memories is of a friend, worn out and angry at the age of twenty-nine, pregnant for the fifth time, walking in and shaking a bottle of oral contraceptives triumphantly. "If the Pope wants to feed and raise any more, fine," she said. "But I've had it. I can't take it any more."

By 1967, Professor Charles Westoff of Princeton University found that 51 percent of all American Catholic women were using contraceptives. But there wasn't much comfort in being part of the larger crowd when you had the standard, highly developed Catholic conscience. That was certainly true of Dorine and Bert.

They are the only couple of the six profiled who had their first child within the first year of marriage. After talking to many families, I've become convinced that postponing the first child is one of the most critical decisions a couple can make if they hope to be rocking together on the front porch at the age of seventy-five. Time and again, early parenthood seems to derail a relationship. (I, too, sat at my parents' kitchen table on my first wedding anniversary with a baby in my arms, staring at a ceremonial piece of frozen wedding cake, barely able to comprehend the fact I was now a wife, not a daughter, let alone the mother of this small bundle before me.)

It's an Everyman experience. "We never had time to get to know each other," said an ex-Catholic accountant, father of four, one evening over three gin and tonics. His wife had left, the children gone with her, and of what moral good, he asked bitterly, is it now that they had faithfully avoided birth control?

When Dorine and Bert pull the sheets up over themselves at night, they still take the Catholic Church with them. Sex is infrequent, quick, devoid of experimentation or joy. They have, and this is much in their favor, recently begun to attend a marriage encounter program. The best thing about it, according to Dorine, is hearing other couples talk frankly about their sexual problems. "We're hearing things that make us understand our own attitudes better," she said. "We're almost all Catholics in our group. I feel freer to speak up, and not be afraid I'll look odd about it."

Part of their complicated mix of guilts over the children involves their eldest son. He baffles Dorine and Bert. Maddens them. They do their best, but his refusal to buy the values they've worked so hard to convey hurts them deeply. Dorine clearly sees Bert's manliness at stake in the struggle over making Mark conform, and Bert knows it. He is frustrated because he wants to solve the problem of this eldest child by getting him out of the house, sending him packing, rejecting him as he rejects his parents. But how does one successfully reject one's own child?

It depends in great part on how the situation is defined.

Our rules of what constitutes responsible parenthood are normative, but not necessarily natural.

An uninhibited Cambridge professor, father of three, told me cheerfully, "At age eighteen, we kick our kids out. They're on their own. We'll help support them, help with school problems, any of those things. But it's too much having them at home. After that age, home should be a place you choose to come to, not that you have to come to. All three of them wander in and out, stay awhile, and leave. The place is theirs. But unless they were ill, I would object to them staying."

Another couple, a highway superintendent and his wife from Iowa, weren't as sanguine. They packed off their troublesome sixteen-year-old son to relatives back East, describing the move to friends as "temporary." But they felt uneasy. They felt like "bad" parents. So they brought him back. It strikes me as ironic that upper-middle-class parents have for years had the out of sending their children off to private schools when they can't tolerate them at home. No such socially acceptable route is available to most working and middle-class families. Dorine and Bert know themselves well enough to realize they couldn't tolerate the solution of sending Mark packing. Even though they have managed major changes in their views on such issues as the Vietnam war and contraception, they see themselves realistically as conformists. They consider themselves more liberated than they really are at times ("We witnessed the wedding of a Jewish friend last month," Bert said at one point, obviously proud of his own ecumenicism), but on the whole, they do know themselves.

They have more confidence in their ability to bargain

with each other now than when the children were young. But the problem in this marriage is not that of one partner demanding more power for himself. It is that Dorine is demanding that Bert assume more power and make the decisions about their son which he doesn't feel equipped to handle.

I do wonder how different life would have been for Dorine and Bert if they had not had children, for there are wide contrasts between them and childless couples I interviewed.

Angus Campbell of the University of Michigan maintains that marriages with no children are happier. Clearly, the more people added, the more complex a marriage gets. "It's a geometric progression," said a friend of mine, new to the ranks of motherhood at the age of thirty-two. "Six months ago Phil and I were two people with two people's problems, but now, with the baby, the tension, the complications, the sheer logistics of life have gone off the chart for us." And although, particularly in working-class marriages, children may keep two people together, I've seen a number of instances, including the Broskys, where their presence has diminished the marital relationship.

Some childless couples remain so because they are totally, almost coldly, convinced their marriages couldn't take the strain. One woman, moving up rapidly in the management ranks of an advertising firm, turned herself into a working dynamo after discovering she was pregnant. No one knew, except her husband, and when the company wanted to send her East on a ten-week training program she decided to go. "I lived in a motel and worked ten, eleven hours a day," she said calmly. "I never read up on anything about pregnancy, and when my feet began swelling up, I said, 'What's happening?' And my friends said, 'Put your feet up, baby, and go see a doctor.' Well, I didn't. I didn't have the time. My blood pressure was way up, though I didn't know it then. I took those little pep pills you use to lose weight, and I felt so sick I could barely drag through the day. I *had* to stick with that program."

She did. By the time she saw a doctor, she was in her seventh month, and shortly afterward delivered a stillborn infant. This woman was hardly ignorant of how to take care of herself. She knew what she was doing. "At first I felt loss," she said. "And then I felt an enormous sense of relief." She measured out each word: "I did not then and I do not now want to put the strain of parenthood on my marriage."

Another woman underlined what that strain meant to her with a brutal touch. "My husband is wonderful to me, and I love him very much," she said. "But he's self-centered, happiest out on the golf course on weekends, totally restless at home. That's okay with me. But what kind of marriage would we have if I had a baby? He wouldn't be a good father. I certainly wouldn't want him to be the father of *my* children. So I'm not planning to have any."

If these are contemporary attitudes, why do married couples still go ahead and have children?

Actually, fewer and fewer do. In 1960 one fifth of all women under thirty who had ever been married had not borne a child. By 1970 it was one fourth, and by 1974 it was one third. Millions of young American couples are "postponing" their babies. They are savoring their freedom, enjoying double incomes, and worrying about overpopulation. So they say "later" to each other, "later" to their parents and friends and after a while, "later" has a way of becoming "never." Right now, the first wave of "maybe later" young couples are reaching the age level where they must decide, or else have time make the decision for them. (This problem has triggered so much indecision and agony that Dr. Elizabeth Whalen, a demographer and ecologist, has started one of the country's first pre-parenthood counseling services for the "maybe later" people in New York City.)

But it still takes great determination to resist the societal attitudes which demand that couples who want to be considered respectable and normal start pushing baby carriages. Americans are at least consistent in their ambivalences, according to the polls: they approve of zero population, but disapprove of couples who remain childless.

If it's a tough decision now not to have children, what was it like for couples of the fifties?

The childless couples I talked with (or as anti-parenthood Ellen Peck, author of *The Baby Trap,* calls them, "child-free") usually described the decision as one made in fragments. "At first we postponed having a baby because I was in graduate school," said the editor of a large Midwest newspaper chain. "Then we were moving around too much. Then my wife began moving ahead in her job—" He shrugged. "Now, if she suddenly said she wanted a child, I would be very surprised. I know I don't want to."

Very few of these couples express regrets. In all cases, the wives are working, and they are reluctant to jeopardize their careers at this late date to start families. One woman, offered a new and challenging job reorganizing the features department of a major newspaper, told her husband cheer-fully, "Look, for the next two months, you'll hardly see me. We'll be strangers. I'm going to work until midnight if I feel like it, sleep at my desk if I feel like it, but I'm going to get this operation moving." He didn't hesitate a second to offer approval. "Now how in the hell," she said to me, "could I have tackled this job if I was raising children?"

The childless couples I interviewed tend to be perfection-ists. They want to live in environments that are centrally calm—nobody leaving jam on the refrigerator door, no-body getting dirt all over the white hallway rug—in large part because they lead rapidly paced lives outside the home. They also are unapologetic about the "selfish" label. "I went through that," said a seventh-grade schoolteacher from Indiana. "But the pressures weren't as strong as they might have been, because at least I'm teaching kids. I look at the kids I teach, and I'm glad we never had children. Ten years ago, I fussed with them about leaving candy wrappers on the lawn. Now I come in in the morning, and find prophylactics all over the place." She shook her head. "All I have to do is get them picked up. I don't have to deal with what's happening and I don't want to—I don't understand it."

For some couples, the fear is that only without children will the center of their marriage hold. "If my wife got pregnant, we'd end up getting a divorce," said the news-paper editor calmly. "We've got a good balance now, but that would blow the whole thing." The reverse of that was also expressed: remaining childless leaves more freedom to dismantle the marriage without complications.

At its best, a marriage without children reflects strong

friendship and involvement that isn't as easily possible in the world of boy scout meetings and squabbles over school grades.

One of the most impressive of such marriages I ran across was in California:

Lisa is something of a Doris Day type, with gold-red hair. She is fond of small, outrageous gestures—like wearing a bright gold felt cowboy hat at her desk. She is forty-four, bouncy, gregarious, cheerfully Jewish: "Marrying into goyim, I learned ways of maintaining distance, but it's not really me." Her husband is a doctor and she is a college professor. He is a quiet conservative and she is a woman whose emotions sprawl and explode and fill a room. They lead separate professional lives, have been married twenty years, and are very happy they never had children.

"We're really cronies," said Lisa. "I don't think we're like ordinary married couples. We're more like kids playing at it. I tell him, 'You're Peter Pan and I'm Wendy,' and maybe that's not the best adjustment in the world, but it works for us." She leaned back in her chair and let out a deep laugh from the belly. "Without him, I'd fall into a million pieces of shit."

Her husband John doesn't look much like Peter Pan. He is a worker, a stolid man with both feet planted on the ground at all times, who says with a twinkle in his eye, "Being married to Lisa is like walking around with a snake in my pocket." They are clearly opposites, two people who have programmed out the strain of children from their lives, convinced that gives them more strength to tolerate each other's differences.

Unlike most couples without children, they have a basis

for comparison. "We had this bad time when a friend went to Europe and his oldest daughter came to live with us for a year," said Lisa. "That kid was something else. She came, fifteen and a half years old and steaming. I couldn't believe it. I had lived with that family years before, and I wiped her ass when she was four and mopped when she threw up, and carried her everywhere. We didn't know we were going to get a little Lolita off the plane. She asked what the rules would be. Could she smoke and drink? I was flabbergasted, and my husband said, "Well, absolutely not. Now if you have any other questions, feel free to ask.'" Lisa's voice grew tight with anger. "We couldn't get a night's sleep for a year. That kid would have had us divided and conquered if she could." Not many parents would feel free to make such a statement so openly. They might resent the children or fear their influence on the marriage, but in our carefully fictionalized child-loving society (which ignores, for example, the problem of parental child abuse), that kind of complaining just isn't acceptable. Most couples I know still implicitly believe that what their children are reflects what they are. "So thoroughly are we taken up with the importance of raising children that a subconscious but nonetheless widespread standard of judging people is by their children," writes Joseph Epstein.

But something else is stirring in the breasts of American parents. Columnist Ann Landers casually threw out a question to her thousands of readers recently: "Was parenthood worth it?" The response, she said, was staggering. Seventy percent of the 10,000 readers who wrote back answered with a loud "No."

Clearly, a lot of people never were suited for parenthood and shouldn't have had children. But it's hardly likely all of those negative responses came only from people incapable of the job of child rearing. Joanne Woodward, the actress, put it frankly in an interview: "I had a baby because that's what you did, right? You had a baby. I didn't know anything about it; I was scared to death. I still don't like children. I don't like children. I DON'T . . . LIKE . . . CHILDREN!" Then she added, "I like my own children."

An uncertainty, if not downright disillusionment, about parenthood has set in since the mid-sixties. A baby becomes a fussy three-year-old, a spoiled four-year-old, a moody adolescent, a rebellious teenager. He fights with his brothers and sisters, smokes dope, drives the family car too fast, costs a fortune to educate. And he never, never comes with a money-back guarantee. Erica and Brian Tate, Alison Lurie's battling couple in *The War Between the Tates,* go from worshipping the ground their children crawl and walk on to viewing them as "the monstrous lodgers." They become, Erica reflects sadly, two people she hardly knows: "In a way it is a relief that nothing now remains to remind her of her beloved, lost Jeffo and Muffy." Is it any wonder so many parents of the sixties are enrolling in Parent Effectiveness Training classes?

And there's more. I met couples who expressed deep frustration that nonparenthood as a life style is beginning to gain popularity when it's too late for them. They look at their children with something more than disillusionment. They look at them as if they wish they could throw them back. In these cases, I have wished today's more honest attitudes toward parenthood had emerged twenty years earlier.

Back in the fifties we needed somebody to stand up and announce the Emperor had no clothes. "That's why I wrote my book," said Ellen Peck, author of *The Baby Trap*. "Somebody had to stand up for those of us who wanted no part of having children. It isn't irresponsible at all to choose against a family. Why do people still feel they have to apologize?"

Why, indeed? But on the other hand, how do you defend parenthood these days? The pleasures of being a parent are hard to convey. How do you tell someone fearful of diapers and soaring college costs that a child is also a window on a life larger than any one individual can experience, that the sheer complexity of that child with the runny nose and $1,500 mouthful of orthodontic work is a joy?

It isn't easy. "I'm very glad I had my children young," said one woman thoughtfully. "I would not want to be without them. But today I wouldn't dream of risking all that trauma again, and I don't blame people who would rather skip the risks than enjoy the pleasures."

Dorine and Bert Brosky love their children. They would be lost without them. Life as they have structured it would cease to mean much if they were gone, but the seesaw between burden and pleasure seems weighted negatively. Perhaps they would have been better off without children, or at least fewer, but a mistake can be seen as a mistake only in retrospect. Given their particular set of circumstances, it couldn't have worked out differently for the Broskys. So although they at times regret parenthood, they are sensible enough not to make a daily issue of it. They have that regret focused. They haven't fallen into a pattern of blaming each other for a mutual frustration, something I've frequently seen happen.

It's easy to say that Catholicism is the primary glue of the marriage, but that doesn't sufficiently explain Dorine and Bert's relationship. For although divorce may still be officially unacceptable as a way out for unhappily married Catholics, no Church rule can stay the process of marital disintegration. Once the flood begins, the center doesn't hold. I remember another Catholic couple, proud owners of a beautiful North Shore Chicago home, parents of four All-American–type children, activists in their local parish. They have the classic "everything." But when the fifth pregnancy came, years of bitterness and anger began to seep out and around them, filling their tidy blue-and-white, Wedgwood-cool suburban lives. She lost the baby, but not her anger. He decided on a vasectomy and to hell with Church prohibitions. He marched out of the doctor's office after the operation, thrust the excised tube of flesh in front of her face and yelled, "See? See? Now will you quit blaming me for getting you pregnant and ruining your life?"

Bitter and unhappy. But very Catholic and very married.

So why do Dorine and Bert, these two earnest, hard-working people have a reasonably solid working marriage? Some simple reasons: they share a common disillusionment with their common backgrounds that gives them a common language. They offer each other substantial emotional security. They see themselves changing in a changing world, but each has the other alongside, hanging over the same cliff. They are realistic about the limitations of their lives, much more involved with their own personal standards than with chasing after other people's. In sum, they are committed to staying together in a way that goes beyond religious or cultural or economic ties.

the isolates
Diana and Phil

It was a bitter Minnesota night in the winter of 1957. Diana, on switchboard duty at her sorority house, jumped when she heard the doorbell ring. It wasn't exactly a night for callers, but it was her job to answer and so she did, opening the door slightly, bracing against the wind.

A tall young man with dark bushy hair and fierce, staring eyes stood on the frost-covered steps. They looked at each other for a second, saying nothing. Then Diana shut the door in his face.

She walked back to the telephone desk as a friend watched with amazement. "Sherry," she said to the friend. "Will you go let that man in? I just can't do it."

"I had to close the door on him," says Diana now, eighteen years later. "He looked alien, somehow. Overwhelming. I couldn't stand looking at him for a second longer."

And so began a four-year courtship. From it came another working marriage.

Diana is a woman lushly built, with full breasts and long, heavy hair, who manages the feat of staying soft-voiced

91

even with three children under ten at home. She seems authentically calm at the center. If she were not, the core of this marriage would probably blow apart, because Phil is a forever restless, pacing person. Diana's calmness is partly natural, partly learned. When she sees a problem coming, she moves quickly to defuse it. If her husband is worried or upset, or speaking with great agitation, she sits quietly, making little sounds of sympathy. She does not resent her role. She is traditionally moldable—and yet not moldable. Her intensity, her opinions beyond her husband's concerns are bound up in children. At thirty-seven, she longs to bear at least one or two more, and failing that, she talks of becoming a midwife.

Phil is as intense and fierce now as he was the night Diana shut the door in his face. He rarely smiles fully. He is a man haunted by what he feels is the slow progress of his career, for he is obsessed with "making it." Phil is a novelist. He and Diana and their children are not rich, but they live very well in a woodsy, reconstructed barn in Connecticut, financed by the kind of modest, steady sales that are the dream of many writers.

Not Phil's. He frets and doubts and agonizes and rails against publishers and reviewers and magazines that turn down his fiction. He is intense and compelling and very involved with ideas, but at times he is like a child kicking a tin can down the block, grumping over his dreams of making a best-seller list, determined to hear or see or feel nothing good about himself.

Most people would consider him reasonably successful. He cannot tolerate the possibility. "I'm kind of paranoid, and I know it," he says. His strength, through all the rumblings and grumblings, is Diana, and he knows it. So does she.

Phil and Diana Morris live near the crest of a hill, miles from town, separated from the main road by a curving, rutted path just wide enough for a car, a path that becomes impassable in a snowstorm. They describe themselves as isolated people, deliberately removed from casual friendships—something they boast of, gently.

But on this late September night, that seems incongruous. They are sitting with friends around a redwood table perched at a slight angle on their rolling lot at the back of the house. Children, their own and assorted others, are running around the yard, crawling under the table, shouting, rubbing watermelon-smeared faces in the laps of their mothers. The adults pay them no heed. Elbows up on a table filled with paper plates, chicken bones, and watermelon rinds, they start a lively discussion about busing. But they soon realize they are all against it for the same reasons, and the talk washes into an exchange of other liberal views.

Diana begins the type of under-the-main-conversation chat with a female guest which is a prelude to moving quietly away from the men into a clean-up routine.

Phil looks up. "Hey, we'll get that stuff," he says. Diana smiles, and smooths her hands across the front of her red-and-white striped patio dress, streaked now with grease stains. It has been a convivial evening. Phil starts clearing the plates and cups, and the wives begin collecting their children. It is all very noisy and nice.

As Phil makes his third trip into the house carrying assorted debris, he looks at Diana and displays a quick smile. "Cheating on my wife is putting the dishes into the dishwasher without rinsing them," he says. The guests laugh.

They say goodbye. "See you soon!" "We shouldn't do this so infrequently." "Have a good year . . ." Phil and Diana are standing together at the gate, waving, as the cars pull out. When they turn around, their company smiles look frazzled, worn, and they become brisk and matter-of-fact.

"Phil, you sit down and talk and I'll get the kids in bed," says Diana. In the house, the tired cry of a six-year-old begins to rise into the night air. Phil nods, but he does not sit down. He abstractedly shoves the left-over watermelon rinds to the center of the table, where they remain for the rest of the night.

"I don't know if we have that much to say about marriage," he says, "I don't know if we're the type of people who would be interesting at all." He shrugs. "What do you say? We believe in freedom." He pauses. "And with you here, we'll protect each other." It is a flat, honest statement. Privacy lines will be drawn. We chatter about nothing much until Diana comes back.

Their courtship lasted over four years and was a rocky one, with much time spent apart. The ties seemed so fragile at one point that Phil was convinced only a cat they mu-ana wryly. "So we owned a cat together."

"We weren't liberated enough to live together," says Diana, wryly. "So we owned a cat together."

Where had I heard that before? Ah, the Steins, I thought. "The damned thing got sick and the vet told us we'd have to put it to sleep," says Phil. "We were walking down the street carrying it, trying to decide what to do, and I thought, My God, if the cat dies, what happens to us?"

"We thought it was the end of the world," Diana remembers. "We loved the cat, and the doctors had done absolutely the wrong things for it, and suddenly it got all bound up in *us.*" She laughs. "I guess you wouldn't call that much of a crisis. But it was for us then."

Diana wanted to teach high school English and get married and have children, but there was another side to her back in the fifties. She wanted to roam, to see the world before she settled down. This did not sit well with the forceful, adamant Phil. He had decided to marry Diana, but she did not comply in quite the way he expected.

"I decided to go to Europe for six months," she says. "And I had a real sense that I was making a choice. Given Phil's eligibility and his charm, he could easily have been swooped up by someone, but I really wanted to travel, and there was a lot I wanted to see."

That wasn't the way it was supposed to work out. Both Phil and Diana were very caught up in the romanticism of the fifties, and most of their dating in the first two years was of the special, dress-up kind. Phil came many times to the sorority-house door, and Diana would come down the stairs to meet him in frothy net formals and he would pin a corsage on her dress and they would go off to dance in glittery halls. It was fairy-tale dating.

"I feel we were almost divorced before we got married, because of my trip to Europe," Diana says.

Phil flashes her a look of amusement and slaps at a mosquito. "I waited for you," he says.

"I suppose we weren't as caught up in the romanticism as I've thought," says Diana. "If we had been, we would have gotten married within a year."

"We concentrated on the cat."

"And mutually nursed it back to health."

Phil suddenly laughs, and spreads his arms wide in a quick gesture of frustration. "Look, we're not people who've led very momentous lives," he protests.

"Whatever that means," murmurs Diana.

"Well, it's nothing like 'This may go beyond your wishes, Diana, but I'm having twelve affairs' or, 'Phil, you may not like this, but I'm going to become an astronaut.' We have disagreements and confusions about things, but I don't think we've ever had a horrible crisis." He thinks for a moment. "The worst for me was marrying a non-Jew. That was a major decision."

Phil comes from a family where education and achievement are valued highly, where Judaism is a connecting link between the material and spiritual in far more than an ethnic or cultural way. And yet, though his mother, who is a doctor, and his father, a businessman, were never deeply religious, they didn't want Phil to marry a gentile; they saw it as a dilution. So did Diana's parents, who were Presbyterian.

Says Diana, "I told my mother we were getting married, and she said, 'Wonderful. We'll get the church where you were baptized for the wedding.'"

Says Phil, "I told my parents and they were upset. Then they said it was all right if Diana would convert to Judaism."

They did neither.

"We found a wonderful man who was a Talmudic scholar, and then we wrote our own ceremony," says Diana.

"I don't remember writing our own ceremony," objects Phil.

Diana is unperturbed. "Anyway, it was a very simple ceremony and we were married at the home of a cousin. Everybody finally came around, and accepted our way of doing it."

Diana and Phil lived for the next four years in Boston. They did not start a family. "We were simply not ready," says Diana. "I loved teaching."

Phil finished his doctorate in English literature, and they lived peacefully, with few quarrels. "See?" says Phil. "I told you we weren't momentous."

"Well," says Diana, pursing her lips slightly, "there was the time the school district sued me in court."

Phil instantly bristles with the memory. "God, yes. They persecuted you ferociously."

Diana, caught up in the convulsions of racial strife in the sixties, tried to introduce a Black Studies Day in a small Massachusetts town.

"The school board was very unhappy," she said.

"Bunch of racist pigs!" explodes Phil. He jumps up and begins to pace the lawn. "One of the parents complained she allowed the kids to excerpt a play with four-letter words. The principal calls the cops, and right away this guy comes to the house with a warrant for Diana's arrest."

In retrospect, the incident no longer frightens Phil and Diana, but they are still angry. They were deeply involved in the civil rights movement of the sixties, and their beliefs in liberal causes were total. When Diana—calm, quiet Diana—was accused of teaching obscenity, they were suddenly catapulted to the center of a stage filled with as wrathful a cast as a small rural town could muster. Diana remembers the chain of events more matter-of-factly than Phil.

"What I had done was a criminal offense in that town," she says. "So they took me to court. By that time I was pregnant."

"I went for a walk that morning," says Phil, "and I thought, My God, I could lose this woman! My wife could go to jail with my child in her womb, and there wasn't anything I could do."

"Well, we learned who our friends were," says Diana.

"We sure did," responds Phil, and clearly he feels resentment. "Some of them were great. And then there were the others who just sat back and said things like 'Listen, what can happen? So you visit your wife and child in prison once a week.'"

"As it turned out, the judge decided the excerpt was obscene," says Diana. She shakes her head impatiently, remembering. "He read it in court, out of context, and he made it sound dirty. But he did some hair-splitting thing where he decided I wasn't guilty of introducing the material in class, which I would have had to have done in order to be culpable under the town statute. So that's how it ended."

Phil still broods. "That had a strong effect on me," he says. "It really brought home to me that I was in a partnership. Up to then, I felt I was married. You know, just married. And then I thought, it's more than that. This is my *wife.*" He is agitated and again begins pacing, trying to explain the extent of his feelings.

"With some men, the realization that marriage is a partnership, and a partnership can dissolve, comes when they realize a wife can walk out on you. Being left alone has always been a fear of mine." He pauses. "But that has nothing to do with Diana. What happened to me was I saw how precarious day-to-day living is. I always took for granted that Diana would be with me, and then this horrible thing happened."

"We sort of withdrew into our own private lives after that," says Diana softly.

"We got evicted too," says Phil. He snorts, "Because of our radical leanings, the landlord said. There were too many black folks coming to our house."

Their first child, a son, was born late that summer, and Diana gave up teaching full time. Phil taught part time, but he had begun his first book, and this meant he could spend much of his day at home. Still angry and shaken, he withdrew as much as possible. "We decided we'd eat three meals a day together instead of just seeing each other on weekends. We'd be together, and that was enough. We had each other."

Diana has been listening quietly, periodically making the little assenting noises which she does when Phil becomes excited. But clearly, she has been thinking her own thoughts.

"It's true," she says reflectively. "The court case brought us much closer together. I think we were like a lot of other people. We were spending our lives making an effort to get along with people and collecting friends. You know, he'd bring friends home from work, and I'd bring friends home, and it was all very easy and comfortable. But there was a delusion in it." She leans forward, speaking earnestly. "When you spend that much energy pleasing other people, you don't know each other well enough, in a way. You develop a—a kind of funny numbness to one another, because you're so busy. That hadn't happened to us. But when we realized we were in trouble, we found some of our friends weren't our friends. And that made our social life seem hollow."

Phil says, "We began to see fewer people. We became far less sociable. It was our way of saying, 'Being with one another is enough.' " He turns to Diana. "Don't you think so?"

And this time, she nods.

A new phase of life began for Diana and Phil. They moved to their home in Connecticut and began a pattern of living that revolved primarily around themselves and their family. Diana was soon pregnant again. Phil took one room of the old barn and converted it into an office where he spends much of his working life. He writes in the mornings, wanders upstairs around lunchtime to check the mail and talk to Diana, who is mostly home these days, although she is a substitute teacher at a nearby grammar school. It is a peaceful, unstructured life. And it is also more togetherness than many married couples could tolerate.

"Well, it works for us," says Phil. He looks at Diana expectantly.

"It works for us both," she says evenly, "from Phil's point of view. I mean, it's geared to his routine."

"Diana inevitably gives in to me," concedes Phil.

"I usually feel good about it," she answers.

"We don't have any rules," says Phil. "But there's an understanding. I'll ask her what the day's schedule is, and she'll tell me, and I'll say, 'Can I work these hours without interruption?' And if she agrees, then the burden of making it work is on her." He pauses. "It isn't entirely fair."

Diana looks at him and smiles, but says nothing.

"I try to keep checking with you," he says, his voice faintly edged. "There's no law in this house that you can't go out and work and do what you want to do."

Diana instantly responds to the note of worry in his voice. "I like being home right now," she says. "I always loved teaching. But right now, I like being home."

There is an empty moment, as if what she was going to say hasn't been completed. But Diana is deep in her own thoughts, so Phil picks up the conversation.

"What about your ideas for a new career?" he prods gently.

Diana's face lights up. "I know it seems a bit odd," she says, "but I'm fascinated with the idea of midwifery. I don't think going back to teaching full time is what I want; it just doesn't have the allure it had when I stopped seven years ago. I would like to do other things." She laughs. "Phil and I aren't planners. We really don't have much of an idea of what we want to be doing ten years from now, but when I think about midwifery, well, I have this mental image of myself as a woman in my sixties or seventies, being very happy delivering babies. I've never projected an interest of mine that far ahead in my life before, but this fits into my basic concerns about my family, and my commitments."

Diana looks almost evangelical as she talks. In a sense, she is a woman out of step with her time. She is Earth Mother, a woman untouched by modernism. She loves birthing. When her years for giving birth are over, she wants to be part of the process in a way that not many women would.

"I love children," she says simply.

"Diana does most of the child raising," says Phil.

"They feel very close to you," she says.

What about women's liberation?

"I am liberated," she says matter-of-factly. "I'm doing just what I want to do."

Which is not to say that parenthood came any easier to Phil and Diana than it does to anyone else.

"Having our first child was like a revolution," says Diana. "It turned everything completely around for us. We became caretakers—feeding and nurturing and bedding them. It really changed our lives very much."

There were the tantrums.

"Mine," says Phil. He moves restlessly. "When we moved into this house I thought, My God, what have I got myself into financially? I'm an impetuous, impatient person, and I want to do things *now*. I want to go around the world, I want to be famous. Why in hell do I have to wait? When is something going to happen?"

Phil's mind has moved on to his writing, but Diana, unperturbed, talks again of children, linking the thoughts of this man she knows well with what she is thinking.

"Children turn one's life upside down," she says. "My vital energies have gone into taking care of infants, and that took away a kind of primal focus on Phil."

"That made me feel left out. And then trapped," says Phil. "Kids yelling and screaming are horrible to me, particularly when my stuff is getting rejected. And here I am with all these kids and I have to say to myself, Okay, Phil boy, go down there and earn a lot of money and be creative. Don't forget, you've got to be creative." He looks quickly at Diana. She makes a comforting sound.

"Diana has heard this a lot," he continues. "I bitch and moan, and it isn't good for us."

"I think if the real truth were written about having children, then fewer people would have them," says Diana. "Particularly if a couple has a good marriage and they want to savor it."

There is another unfilled moment of silence. I reflect quickly on the dangers of stereotypes, and mentally I scratch my initial definition of Earth Mother.

There is more to Diana's love of birthing. It is sexual.

"Sex is very important," Diana says quietly. "It is very much part of the caring and nurturing of children. For me, having children increases my—well, my sexual bonding with Phil. When I had our last child, Phil was standing behind me and the doctor was in front of me delivering the baby, and I had a whole new sense of Phil as a man; it was wonderful—he was part of the baby and the baby was part of me." Overwhelmed for a moment, Diana stops.

Phil looks at her. "You want to know what is irreplaceable about this marriage?" he says. "I'll tell you. Her."

"I say exactly the same. Phil."

"But I'll tell you, if we're honest—" Phil pauses. "Well, having kids didn't make our sex life any better. We get interrupted a lot."

"It doesn't cause us big problems," says Diana. "That's because we feel our sex life takes in the whole picture—the way we treat one another. It's the touching and the caring in little ways that matters. I don't think having children needs to have a negative effect on one's sex life." She looks quickly to Phil for affirmation. He hesitates briefly, and nods.

"I'm thinking about what's irreplaceable," he says. "My God, the kids are, too."

"I hope we never have to face the death of one of our children," says Diana.

"We have plenty of fights." Phil says this flatly. "They're bitter, sarcastic, sardonic personal spats. I play Russian actor and Diana goes into her Danish denial retreat."

"But in about an hour it all looks silly," says Diana.

Phil smiles at his wife. "We don't keep book on each other," he says. "The worst thing for a marriage is total recall."

What digs in the most? What angers? What festers—for a little while?

"Mainly sometimes the fact that marriage can get overwhelming with its daily catastrophes," says Diana. "You know, the burdens of paying for the house and taxes and doing the housework and getting food on the table. Sometimes I feel burdened too much. Sometimes I think it's the other way around. It's Phil who has to be creative and be the breadwinner, and even when I'm working part-time teaching he's the one really supporting us in the style we want. That's an incredible monkey to have on your back." Diana's face puckers into a small frown. "I'm responsible for buying things," she says. "I don't think I get us into holes with charge accounts and stuff—but living is so expensive."

"Listen, Di," scoffs Phil, "if I didn't go out and buy you dresses once in a while, you'd never wear a new one."

"Phil, I *enjoy* sewing."

He waves his hand in a quick, dismissing gesture. "I know that. The extravagance of our life style is mine."

They both look toward the house, obviously thinking of mortgages.

And that brings them to Phil's ambitions.

"When I get mad at Di, it's usually because I don't feel she's giving me enough support," he says. He shifts in his chair. "It's wholly neurotic, and it doesn't fester. But I can feel pretty sorry for myself at times." Again he pauses. "A lot of it is because my mother and father have been so successful. Particularly my mother. Terribly successful." He laughs, a quick, sharp sound. "The standards for success in my family are very high."

People used to think it was cute when Mrs. Morris would take time out from her busy practice as Dr. Morris and go to Phil's baseball games and then never be able to remember who was the pitcher and who was the catcher and what was the point of it all, anyway? There she would be, loyal and cheering, in the dusty stands on a Saturday afternoon and people told Phil he was pretty lucky to have a mother like that. "So, okay," he says. "If she cared so much, why didn't she learn what I was doing?"

A long time ago. But the question lingers.

"I want to break through," says Phil. His voice is hungry. "I was talking to an editor last week, a very nice man, and I told him I wished I had a book ready for him, and he said, 'What you need is something to break through with.'"

Phil's frustration palpitates in the air. "A friend of mine just published a book. Terrific success. He reached that moment in his life where he broke through. Then look at other writers. There was a moment in Studs Terkel's life when he broke through. Take a guy like Philip Roth—he's broken through. And what's her name Rossner—that Mr. Goodbar or whatever—and Linda Wolfe who wrote this book on women having affairs. That broke through. So now if a book on sex is reviewed in the *New York Times*, Linda Wolfe is apt to be asked to review it. That means you're known. It can be irrational. It can be going to a lot of cocktail parties and having an editor say, 'Hey, you'd be a good person to review this book,' and suddenly you're in."

Diana breaks in. "I can't do anything about it. I know how hard it is, but I can't help you. All I can do is be empathetic, to feel what I feel, which is a total sympathy, and hope you don't get too discouraged."

Phil seems to snap back from somewhere. "God, you help a lot. My greatest fear is that you'll leave me."

They look at each other, and neither looks away.

"I try to be thoughtful," says Phil.

"You are," she comforts.

Diana turns toward me. "I love what Phil writes," she

says. "Maybe I should be able to be more critical, but I think it's great. But he's so hard on himself. He's his own worst critic."

"Look, in the past three years I've had over a thousand rejection slips," says Phil.

Diana closes her eyes briefly. "It's so hard," she murmurs.

Phil sighs. "Oh, well, it's a random world out there. I've had stories turned down thirty-five times and then accepted by the thirty-sixth magazine."

He brightens. "There's a good side. Nothing's predictable. We like to live that way."

Diana nods. "We're closing up the house and traveling on a grant next year," she says.

The frustration in the air lifts. "You can see that I'm obsessed with my career. But I'm not obsessed with my marriage," says Phil.

He looks toward Diana, adding, "I don't mean I take it for granted. Well—I do. In the sense that it's always there. There is a tremendous constancy about Diana." He smiles and tosses off what is obviously a favorite joke.

"She's the wife of my first marriage."

"Phil, I've never liked your saying that. It has a bite. An edge. I don't like it."

His eyes widen. "Really? I'm sorry."

Diana's flash of resolve is unsettling.

Phil launches into something of a thumbnail sketch of himself; one that somehow seems geared to obliquely re-assure.

"I'm a very predictable person," he says. "I don't go to parties and get drunk. I don't even smoke grass any more. I'm going to write a book on my private life and tell the world that cheating on my wife means putting the dishes in the dishwasher without rinsing them first." He pauses.

Diana smiles at another joke heard once again.

"It's a very straight life," he continues. "There's nothing I like to do that Di doesn't like to do, too."

"Well—" she begins.

"Oh, sure," he says. "There are certain things she wants to do and I'm not interested and I feel free to say, 'Go ahead, and leave me out.' She feels free to do the same thing when I've got something I want to do that doesn't get her all excited."

Diana smiles. "We've got a philosophy, I guess, but we've never really discussed it."

"If you hadn't come tonight, we probably never would have," says Phil.

Phil moves closer to the table, puts his elbows up, ignoring the watermelon seeds. "We don't try to share everything," he says.

"Partly because we're together physically so much," adds Diana.

"I don't think every single space and every single crevice in me needs to be open to Diana," he says. "That's killing. I get to keep secrets. About me. About you. There are certain things I know about you I would never divulge to anyone else."

Diana answers, "There are certain things about you that I would never divulge to anyone else."

"We've watched our friends crap on each other, as if it's funny," says Phil. "And look at these women comics—Joan Rivers and Phyllis Diller with her jokes about Fang. Why do people defame or malign the person they're married to?"

"It's sad," says Diana.

"It's a crock," says Phil.

"It's true about not keeping book on each other," Diana says, thinking. "If I'm substitute-teaching, Phil takes care of the children, empties the garbage, and that sort of thing. Maybe one week he'll work seventy-two hours on his writing, but that doesn't mean he owes me time."

"Sometimes it comes out in our arguments," Phil says.

"That's true," Diana replies. "Maybe it's good."

"Sure it is. We can't always live with a silent agreement."

Diana again becomes thoughtful. "Phil, remember Dave talking about his wife last week? He said, 'You know, she makes few demands, but she has a lot of expectations.' I thought that was very perceptive."

"It's hardest to respond to those silent expectations," she continues. "That's one of our problems. Unless you say something, I don't always respond."

"Yeah. I do the same. Then things get lopsided."

Diana spreads her hands, palms up. "But who can meet another person's silent expectations all the time?"

Phil laughs. "Can't. That's why we've got to work at not keeping book. Look, what about women's liberation? Maybe you're keeping book on me."

Diana shakes her head. "I do what I want to do," she says.

"I guess after all these years of marriage, you wouldn't be holding a bunch of things in, would you?" His voice teases, lightly.

Diana responds to the question within the question. "I'm happy," she says. "I don't think any movement could really affect anything as deeply rooted as my marriage to you. That gets proven or disproven between you and me." She pauses. "I'm impressed with what women have been doing, and I believe in a lot of it. But it just doesn't personally affect me."

"No one's ever sentenced you to anything." His voice still teases.

Diana laughs. "Gosh, no."

The night has deepened into morning, and mosquitoes are rising from the damp grass, distracting, irritating. Phil scratches absently at a bite, and says reflectively, "I've been thinking about marriage tonight more than I usually do. It's a lot like health. What does it mean to say that you're feeling healthy? It means you're without pain. You don't think about your teeth unless you feel pain. When your teeth hurt you're thinking about them every twenty seconds until you get to a dentist. I don't think much about my marriage. I count on it. I know it's going to be there." He looks at Diana. "I know she's going to be there."

Diana holds out her hand to Phil across the watermelon rinds. "Wherever you are, that's my center. That's it."

When I leave, it is with a copy of Phil's latest novel, pressed upon me gently by Diana. "It's really a wonderful book," she says. "We have high hopes for this one." Phil looks away, a bit embarrassed, but still uneasily proud. I ask him to sign my book, wish them well, and say goodbye. Phil's intensity has cooled, but he seems thoughtful, a little depressed. Diana takes his hand without comment, and to-gether they walk me to the gate.

It would be hard not to admire a woman like Diana. In a curious way, she reminded me of the nuns who taught me as a child; not in a physical sense (no black robes and veil for Diana), but in the serene way she lives within the context of a commitment to something totally outside of her self. That "something," of course, is Phil. To him, she offers all loyalty, trust, and fidelity. He returns it, in great part. But admiring him is tougher.

I found myself alternating between liking Phil and being annoyed with his intensity, his overwhelming needfulness. He has taken the center in this marriage and holds it. Diana allows him that center because, fortunately, she doesn't need it as much as, say, Jan Stein. (If Jan Stein were married to Phil Morris, it wouldn't be a union; it would be an explosion.) Phil takes the lead in everything, whether it is discussing her career or the children or their friendships. This keeps the balance of power in the marriage tipped in his direction; almost more important, it keeps Diana's attention fully on him. That makes Phil come across at times as a dominating child.

There seems to be no way for Phil Morris to feel reasonably satisfied with himself. He wins a prestigious grant to study overseas for a year, and only reluctantly acknowledges it. He publishes books that don't make the book club lists, but do get positive reviews, and he yearns for more. Much more. He keeps upping the ante. The way he operates would probably drive most women crazy.

But not Diana. And that's because he reflects back to her an image of self as sexual Earth Mother that she needs very much. Diana may have chosen midwifery as a future career goal solely out of her desire to serve in some capacity at birthing, but I suspect something else is operative: midwifery is almost the only profession she could have chosen that wouldn't threaten her husband, other than teaching. She has adjusted herself to his expectations, in part. I say "in part" because those crucial adjustments also serve her "I am a good person" needs. In other words, Diana is not some kind of acquiescent scapegoat in this marriage. She is getting as well as giving, and so far, the balance works.

This certainly isn't a marriage between equals, in any popularly definable sense. But what does that mean? A better word is reciprocity. "What each member of the duality gets from marriage may not be the same," writes Elizabeth Janeway. "But it should be sufficient of a reward for each to continue choosing the relationship even when it kicks up difficulties." Well, Phil and Diana are apparently getting sufficient mutual rewards. Nonequality hasn't kicked up many difficulties.

It would be a mistake also to think of sweet, complacent Diana as weak. With some internal sense of timing that those who rush through courtship and into marriage apparently lack, she had the good sense and instinct to suspend their courtship and travel, not only to leave Phil free to resolve his ambivalence, but to indulge herself. "There were places I wanted to see and things I wanted to do before I got married," she said. Did she worry about the risk of losing Phil? Yes, she did. But she had enough of a balance of need and independence to take the chance. And that may have played an important part in how their marriage is working.

Psychologist Bernard Murstein has a theory that courtship consists of three critical stages. First comes the stimulus stage, where two people meet and respond solely to visual, auditory, and reputational clues. (She's got a lovely smile, she is witty, she is well liked by her friends. He is tall, he is well informed, he is a successful doctor.) Next comes the value stage, the time when two people become more careful in the silent process of weighing assets and deficits. It's the most important, according to Murstein, because they are trying to discover if they are compatible, and it's a tricky business figuring out what compatibility means. Common interests? Not really. Phil's passionate civil libertarianism used to bore Diana to tears. Her attention would wander, and although she made a conscientious effort to pay attention to Phil's opinions and declarations, she never assumed she could manufacture compatibility.

The tolerance of the foibles of two separate personalities doesn't go much beyond a cosmetic acceptance until the third stage of courtship, the point where each person has clearly defined expectations for the other, and roles are established. Unfortunately, by the time many couples reach this point, they are already married, committed to a relationship fondly assumed to be static, which will instead always be in process; committed to a set of silent expectations that will most likely never be fully met. It's one of the many Catch-22's of marriage. Diana Morris avoided it by hopping a plane for Europe, taking a chance with time.

Sexually, Phil and Diana enjoy each other. Diana, speaking later and very matter-of-factly, said, "I love it. Partly I find the idea of maybe getting pregnant each time very erotic." If there are problems in this area, and at times there are, they come from Phil's nervous temperament. He is more likely to fall into bed at night, still immersed in anxiety over his writing. Diana, belying her outward passivity, will initiate sex gently. "I don't demand," she said. She is a toucher, a brow-smoother. She is very adroit at sending signals to her husband, including her choice of clothes to wear at home, which often display her large breasts. Phil enjoys talking about his wife's sexuality as it connects to other things, particularly her maternalism. This, for him, is the erotic combination, the one he needs most. The lack of a maternal, nurturing mother has probably fed that need.

I see some interesting parallels between this marriage and another one, that of a West Coast corporation lawyer and his wife, where the feeding of neurosis and need are reversed: she, bursting with anger and energy, has been to all outward appearances the perfect housewife and mother for fifteen years. She plans everything. Dinner is always served precisely at six o'clock, and if anything perishable —milk, mayonnaise—sits out on the table for more than twenty minutes, she throws it away. She spends hours cleaning and polishing and directing her husband in his many household chores. He never acts angry or annoyed. Some of their friends see him as something of a neighborhood saint.

Their marriage has worked for fifteen years because he has an image of himself as the family rock—the pivotal point of constancy and security for his wife's neurotic needs. But the cracks are beginning to show, for she, after five years of therapy, is beginning to understand and break away from her neurosis. She doesn't need programmed attentiveness from her husband any more. She's ready to hang up her apron, give her children more freedom and go find a job. In other words, she's ready to grow, to move on, and he isn't, which, as Nena and George O'Neill point out in *Shifting Gears,* is a serious marital deadlock. "I don't know what's going to happen," she said, driving much too fast down a coast highway one afternoon. "I respect him, and I owe him a great debt, but when we talk now, I feel there's a forty-foot-wide gap between us. He doesn't understand who I have become. And I understand all too well now that his constant acquiescence to me made him feel very comfortable, because he didn't have to get involved deeply in the marriage. He doesn't feel things very much."

"It's true, I don't," admitted her thin, balding husband in a quick moment of candor. "I like things just the way they are."

Their experience demonstrates the fact that no matter how tightly woven the mesh of balanced needs can be in a marriage, one partner can unravel the whole thing fairly quickly. That might possibly be in the cards for Diana and Phil Morris, but I doubt it. The difference isn't a better accommodation of each other, particularly, but a sharper awareness of each other. Neither Phil nor Diana remains neutral as a device for self-protection, so this isn't a case of one tennis ball bouncing against a solid, unchanging wall, as is true in the other marriage. And although it is a modern version of the "ideal" classic marriage of husband as activist and wife as stabilizer, Phil does not say, "This is the wife of my first marriage," without challenge. Diana will support him on everything. Almost everything. But this is the husband of her *only* marriage, and when it comes to jokes about that, she is not so accommodating.

They understand each other's tolerance level for outside stress and change. Phil is the one who most wanted the sheltered, removed life they lead now in rural Connecticut, but living there connects directly with their working balance. When Phil acknowledges his insecurities and hungers by saying, "I know my ambition is a bottomless pit," both he and Diana know it is her job to provide the floor, the roof, and the walls.

I left with a respect for their deliberately imposed isolation. Phil and Diana are not fragile people, although they are apprehensive of change that comes too quickly. Consciously or unconsciously, they protect against change from the outside.

What might destroy their marriage? I think, possibly, a sudden, major success for Phil might do it. But only when or if it comes—this is a working marriage of shared affection and need.

And there's more than that. They convey a real understanding of what happens to a relationship when the tyranny of what Diana called the "silent expectations" one person has for another begin to corrode feelings. If Phil works night and day on a book, contributing nothing during that time to the marriage but dirty coffee cups and filled ashtrays, must he finally emerge solicitous, apologetic and filled with plans for a Big Night Out? Or at least offer to put the kids to bed? "He doesn't owe me time," Diana says firmly. She doesn't demand payment for her understanding. Nor does he. "We don't keep book," he says. He means it.

"What is marriage?" a friend of mine asked herself rhetorically one evening. "It's wheels moving under the ground." If so, Phil and Diana come as close as any couple to understanding the machinery.

the commuters
Anna and Jim

ANNA: "Forty percent of me is you."
JIM: "If sixty percent of you were me, my love, we'd both be in deep trouble."

I see Anna for a fleeting second as my plane touches down. She is standing at the solitary landing gate in the dusty sunshine of a wickedly hot August day, holding the hands of two of her children while a third—the tall, restless, thirteen-year-old Angela—stands nearby. Only a few passengers disembark. There are, after all, not many reasons for a crowd to be flying in to this small, downstate Illinois town on a summer afternoon. Classes are over at the state university. All the students have scattered; the teachers are either sequestered, toiling over dissertations, or in Europe, touring monuments and castles. Champaign-Urbana, the home base of the University of Illinois, is, for the time being, just one more nondescript town sitting isolated out on the Illinois plain.

"Hi," Anna says as I walk toward the gate. Her voice is brisk and fresh, in contrast to her wilted appearance; the voice of a very-together, take-charge, "bring the report in this moment, please" woman. This is the Anna I remember. Her brown hair, knotted in a coil at the back of her head, is pulled so tightly it strains from her skin. She is wearing a Sears, Roebuck special—a flowered cotton housedress. It is very different from the suits I have seen her wear. She looks extraordinarily domestic.

She sees my glance. "I know," she says. "I don't look like a high-powered academic type today. Just a housewife."

I am introduced to Angela, who tosses her hair to the wind and a smile at me at the same time, and to the boys: Joseph, who is eleven and dark and solemn, and Jeffrey, who is ten and giggly. They ask questions and poke each other and laugh, and we all feel self-conscious.

"I'm glad you came," Anna says abruptly. "I don't think you'll regret it. Jim and I think we have some things to say that matter—to us, anyway."

She laughs suddenly as we cart luggage to the station wagon. "Wow, what a marriage we've got!"

The last time I had seen Anna Lowell was many months before, on a cold and bleak Chicago evening over a fettucine dinner in one of those strangely neutered suburban restaurants decorated mostly in red plastic. The setting almost did in our conversation. I knew Anna, not well, as a political scientist making a respectable name for herself locally. She had published a book; she appeared on panels; gave speeches. But she wasn't interested that night in discussing political trends. She wanted to talk about other things: love and sex and children and marriage—all of it together, and what it meant for her.

Anna belonged to that small number of women whose careers led them to one of the newer marital arrangements of the seventies: the commuter marriage. She and her husband, Jim, had been commuting for six years; he, living in Florida working for a flourishing real-estate-development firm, and she in Illinois, teaching and writing at the state university. The children lived with her. Every two weeks Jim came home for a weekend. On holidays the family went to visit him. It was the pattern of their lives, and as such, it was normalcy.

"Nobody else ever thought so," said Anna, staring at her fettucine.

Jim and Anna were then at a crossroads. He was changing jobs, leaving Florida—to come back to Illinois? Or to take another job offered in New York?

"I don't know," she said, looking at the elderly Italian waiter who would not stop fussing over us. "I don't know if I want to be married in the traditional way. Maybe I need to be away from him more than I am with him. Maybe he needs to be away from me more than with me." She shook her head. "I think we either have the best marriage in the world—or the worst."

We talked of loneliness and belonging, of fidelity and affairs, of things that hurt and things that should be concealed. We talked of privacy—of going to bed when one feels like it, alone if one so chooses; of the luxury of not consulting; of not feeling obligated to consider another person when one wants to climb a mountain instead of going to the supermarket.

We talked, really, of the independence of being alone, and we talked also of the pleasures of commitment. For that's really what Jim and Anna were deciding between.

A month after that dreary dinner, they made their decision. Jim didn't go to New York. He came back to Illinois.

And now it was months later, and they had invited me to come see this working marriage, and glimpse perhaps what it meant to them.

The old station wagon turns off the airport road and bounces along a narrow gravel street pocked with holes. "Sorry about this," Anna says with a cheerful wave of her hand, "but it's the shortest route and I've got dinner cooking." Our conversation is light and general and I think about how much calmer Anna looks: the tight lines I remember between her brows have smoothed out; her hands are relaxed on the wheel; her nails are no longer bitten short.

"Are you really staying the whole weekend?" asks Jeffrey.

"If you can stand having me around," I answer.

"But why?" he persists.

"Jeffrey, I told you our guest was staying until Sunday. Now you be polite," Anna says, her voice edged.

I am now defined as something of a mystery.

We turn onto a street of typical development homes, three styles alternating down an undulating block of spindly trees and yellowed but neatly edged lawns. It isn't the type of neighborhood I had imagined.

The house is at the end of the block. Waiting for us, fiddling self-consciously with a lawn sprinkler, is a tall, almost gaunt man of about forty, with thinning hair and a tight, careful smile.

He stretches out his hand in a formal hello. His eyes are nice, but not warm. He is, I suspect, the type of man who prefers life not to come too highly seasoned; a man who will sit silently and smoke a cigarette while others argue passionately over politics or sex or religion because, basically, he doesn't care about that many things.

And this is all true, which, later, he readily admits.

"I would have called you sooner," Anna had said over the phone. "But Jim is a very private person, and I didn't want to invite you here unless he wanted it as much as me. He does now. I'm sure."

I wonder about that as we enter the house. Jeffrey is holding something out to me, a delighted grin on his face. It is a snake, and I jump away.

"Jeffrey!" Jim shouts. "Get that damn snake out of here and don't bring any of them in!"

The snake goes, and so does Jeffrey, and so does the atmosphere of awkwardness. Jim is rueful as he explains about Jeffrey's snake collection. He and Anna tell me some of their favorite snake-on-the-loose stories, and everything is okay.

Jim begins mixing drinks, and Anna starts pulling pots and pans out of the cupboard, readying dinner. I climb up on a kitchen stool covered with cat hairs and we chat—about the kids, about the weather, about the house.

"This dump," Jim says scornfully.

That is strong, but I would probably say the same if I lived there. To be from Los Angeles is to know how fragile this typical, thin-walled, tackily constructed development house can be. You know the plumbing breaks down frequently, even if the fixtures are all a fashionable blue. You know a door slammed upstairs in anger will rattle the glasses in the kitchen. It is a cardboard home, but it is the kind you buy cheap and sell dear, just as long as you pour cement outside of the sliding glass doors that always stick and call it a patio; just as long as you plant trees and bushes and call it privacy. Jim and Anna will hang on to it and later sell without shedding a tear. They are not very attached to their possessions.

Anna is hunting for a fly swatter, hunting diligently, murmuring, "I know it's in a strange place," and apologizing for the flies. I watch one get stuck in some jam on the counter.

"I'm not really a housekeeper," Anna says with a rueful look at the jam.

"No, but boy, are you organized," says Joseph, pointing out to me a complicated chore chart pasted on the refrigerator. "Do you know," he says, with exasperated pride, "that Mom keeps an in-basket *at home?*"

Anna has been working for most of her married life, and the signs of a woman juggling a number of hats are everywhere: the cupboards are lined with instant Kraft cheese-and-macaroni dinners; there is a half-written book review for a journal rolled up next to the toaster; there is a large crayoned note on the refrigerator saying "I NEED SOME PANTS!" and signed "Jeffrey."

The kids point all this out to me. They are proud of their mother.

There is a sense of something new happening within this noisy, cheerful family of five. The children scramble around this unfamiliar unit of father and mother in the kitchen. Periodically Anna or Jim will order them out from under foot. "They won't leave us alone," says Anna at one point, exasperated. "I guess it's because having us both here at dinner time is still a novelty."

Jeffrey brings his father a broken airplane; Joseph discusses his report card; and Anna and Jim respond with a mix of alacrity and irritation. They still feel jumpy with the newness of it all. Old routines and habits must be remolded, somehow shared.

Anna is standing at the stove, cooking mushrooms and zucchini, waving away the flies. She plunks a lid down on the pan.

"Last time I put a lid on that stuff, I wondered if it was a good idea," Jim says offhandedly.

She smiles. "When you cook, you cook," she retorts. "When I cook, I cook."

The lid stays on. There is no further comment.

The hot August sun finally sets, and the breezes blow across the tiny outdoor patio. Dinner is over, and the dishes are done. The children are sent to bed with a mixture of pronouncements from Jim ("Get to *bed!*") and cajolements from Anna ("You can take the TV in for a little while"), and finally it is quiet. Jim opens a bottle of wine and we move to the den, an almost luxurious room, furnished with good leather pieces bought when Jim and Anna had more money than they do now. Anna curls her feet up onto her chair; Jim, looking self-conscious again, gives his wife a quick pat on the shoulder and settles himself into a big black leather chair. We talk for hours, and eventually finish off two more bottles of wine.

Growing up was a lonely experience for Anna, as it was for Jim. They come from adjoining small towns in Iowa. Each was an only child. Each lost a father. Each was raised by a widowed mother without money. Each was very bright, and each won scholarships to prestigious Eastern universities.

It was probably likely they would come together at some point, if only to compare experiences. But many things happened before that.

Anna's mother, a timid, untrained woman, was widowed and left destitute when Anna was five. For three years, she and Anna lived in a small room above a dry-goods store, until her husband's brother, over the objections of his wife, invited them to live at his farm.

Anna loved the farm. She was a dreamy girl, a child who fantasized herself as Ginger Rogers, whirling down a marble staircase in white chiffon into the waiting arms of Fred Astaire. She loved going to Saturday afternoon movies in the little town near her uncle's farm, but her main recreation was books—books read avidly on quiet afternoons out by the barn with no interruptions other than the clucking of the barnyard hens.

Then one Saturday morning, it all changed.

"Mother was out blueberry-picking when a neighbor came slamming through the front door yelling, 'Quick, get a chain!' I didn't understand, but my aunt screamed. She knew what had happened. My uncle's tractor had tipped over on him, and he was going to die if they couldn't lift it off. I remember running out of the house and through the barn, thinking, I'll find a chain! I'll save my uncle! I could find nothing. Nothing at all. So I ran back to the house, but everybody was gone, out in the field. I was afraid, terrified, to look out the window. I didn't want to see my uncle dying."

Later, much later, Anna's mother walked slowly into the house, picked the child up in her arms and started to cry. "He was good to us," she said over and over.

After that, their fragile security collapsed. Anna and her mother had no money. They were on their own again, and Anna's mother went back to scrabbling out a living as a dry-goods clerk. Anna was ten years old.

Jim remembers no dramatic catastrophes, for he comes from a family of cool and reserved people. So when a neighbor came into the house one Christmas Eve and whispered long with his mother, he didn't think much about it. And when his mother told him he was to go with the neighbor, it never occurred to him to ask why, why—on Christmas Eve.

"My father died that evening, but nobody told me. I wasn't expected to ask questions."

The pain came, but it came as a dull, continuing ache, nurtured through the years by his mother. "She was very bitter," says Jim. "She worked in a bakery, because she couldn't do any better, and she worked such long hours, she finally sent me to live for a couple of years with relatives."

Jim and Anna think about their mothers. Both are grateful for the years of hard work devoted to raising them, but they do not feel much love.

"They worked very hard for us," Jim explains. "And we survived because of their efforts. But they are bitter, demanding women."

"Actually," Anna says softly, "they didn't save themselves."

Jim and Anna met in grammar school, an occasion so auspicious for twelve-year-old Anna that she scribbled this entry into her diary: "Met Jim Lowell. Wow!" Jim doesn't remember the event very well. Through the years they saw each other off and on, drifting in and out of friendship circles, moving away to school, coming back home. It was on one of these occasions that Jim got interested enough to write Anna's phone number on a slip of paper. He put it into a bureau drawer, and then forgot about it. He found it one night when he was looking for a date.

"I called her right away," he says.

Anna rolls her eyes at the memory. "By that time, we were so different," she says. "I was deep into the course work for my master's degree at Northwestern. Jim wanted women a little—well, lighter. He was dating stewardesses."

That was in 1957. But in that strange bouncing and mixing of chemistry that no one ever explains very well, Anna was convinced within a few months that she wanted to marry Jim.

"I had been around," she says. "I knew the kind of man who attracted me, and I liked his stability." She laughs. "And a few other things."

Anna and Jim did not have qualms about premarital sex. As Anna puts it, "I discovered religion in college first, knowledge second, and sex third. In each case, one replaced the other."

They played house a little, with Anna, equipped with a fake wedding ring, traveling to Jim's base one weekend when he was in the army. Feeling very daring, they spent three days together in a Missouri hotel as "Mr. and Mrs. Lowell."

But it was not all sweetness and light, as the saying goes.

"Remember that drive back from Wisconsin?" asks Anna.

Jim sighs. "Oh God, do I ever. You really threw me."

It was on that particular drive that Anna told Jim about her previous sexual involvements, in matter-of-fact detail. It wasn't anything he didn't know, really. But on the other hand, it wasn't anything he wanted to know, really.

"I had always kind of assumed I'd marry a virgin," says Jim. "And I told her, that what she was saying wasn't what I had expected."

Anna's eyes flashed. "And I said, 'Well, if sex before marriage with different people is okay for you, why isn't it okay for me?' "

Even in 1957, Jim couldn't come up with a snappy answer for that.

Jim didn't really want to get married and would have been delighted if Anna would have settled for living with him, but that looked like too open-ended a life style in the fifties, even for as independent a woman as Anna.

"I was offered a job in California and asked her if she would come with me, unmarried," says Jim. "She said no. And somewhere along the way, I decided, Well, I was going to have to marry her or lose her. And I knew I couldn't get along without her."

So they were married, in a traditional ceremony complete with white satin gown, floral bouquets and teary-eyed rela-

127

tives. In a way, it was fun, but Anna felt uneasy with the hypocritical underpinnings.

"The minister insisted on counseling us on sex," she says, "and that was irrelevant and awkward. He also kept emphasizing the religious things about marriage, which didn't interest either of us at all."

"Oh, it was a pretty happy occasion," says Jim, "except for a little bit of shit from my mother."

Anna laughs. "She was pretty surprised. She figured Jim was through school and it was time for him to spend more time with her."

Jim stirs restlessly. "I guess it was always kind of difficult for me to accept the fact she never got up and did a little better for herself than she did. I don't know why she couldn't get it into her head that she could be a waitress, sure, but then later she could run a restaurant, but she didn't think that way. I don't know—" He stares into the near distance. "She did a great deal for me, and she was very devoted. For me, she was an obligation." The statement hangs in the air, flat and cold.

Did he feel guilty?

"A little bit," Jim says. "But I tend not to feel too guilty about anything. Maybe I should have given her a little more time, but frankly, I had no interest."

Anna looks reflectively at her husband. "I knew how Jim felt about his mother when we were married," she says. "And his feelings of neutrality continually astonish me. I mean, how anybody could be neutral about Loretta Lowell is beyond me. We were married—how many years?—before she died, and I was so racked with anger and love and hate and guilt for not feeling guilty and everything else." Anna drew a deep breath. "She was a remarkable woman, and she drove us both crazy. Still, Jim, she was your mother. I accept how you feel, but I never will understand it."

Jim nods, and his face stays still. "That's the way it is, I guess," he says.

Early marriage for Jim and Anna followed a standard pattern. Jim went to work and Anna stayed home, keeping house and trying to learn how to cook. She doesn't remember worrying much about using contraceptives, but neither she nor Jim wanted a baby in those early years.

"Marriage was one thing," says Jim. "But the next thing we were expected to do was have a baby, and we weren't ready for that."

Anna nods her head in agreement. "But I got restive," she says. There was too much energy, too many interests being confined in too small a space. "I didn't get the horrible trapped feeling women talk about these days. I didn't sit down and chew my nails and cry about, 'What's wrong with me?' "

"Not you," says Jim, laughing.

"I finished fixing dinner one night, walked into the living room, and told Jim, 'I *hate* this.' I absolutely couldn't stand being cooped up in the house any more."

Jim was not traumatized. "Hell, I knew she was too smart to stick with it for long," he says.

"I think we've always let each other be," says Anna. "We've never had much in common and we probably never will. Certainly our professional lives have gone in opposite directions." She shoots an amused glance in Jim's direction.

"He thinks anybody involved in politics, even research, is absolutely insane, and I've never gotten very excited about" —she flutters her hands for an instant—"whatever the hell it is that you do in business. But from the very beginning, we were able to live together so compatibly. Why, I wonder?"

Jim smiles. "We've always both wanted to sit down and work out a problem, that's why."

Anna, armed with her graduate degree in political science, went hunting for a job. All she could get was a job as a secretary in a marketing research firm which people in the office treated as a joke. "They'd point me out as the secretary with the master's degree," she says. "So I learned. My strategy was to be a lousy secretary and try to get into the professional end of things, which I eventually did. By the time I left that firm, I had a title of some sort that made me more marketable."

Anna spent the next nine years comfortably jumbling together a string of interesting, nondemanding jobs with bearing and rearing her children, without a sense of professional direction, but usually telling herself, "One of these days . . ."

And then one morning she went to the mailbox and opened a letter from her doctor, the kind women get after routine Pap smears that tells them everything is okay. Except it wasn't this time. The report was marked "questionable" and the doctor wanted to see Anna immediately.

"I walked back into the house and I sat down on the bed and thought, My God, I may have cancer. I just may die.

And I thought that Jim would be fine and the kids would be fine and life would go on. The sun would rise and set, and the only person who would really have missed out would be me, because I hadn't done what I wanted to do with my life yet." Anna pauses. "That's what scared me the most."

Shortly after, Anna was operated on for removal of a tumor. And when she came out of the anesthesia, Jim was there to tell her the tumor was benign.

"What better gift can you get than knowing you're not about to die?" she says. "But I decided right then, in that hospital bed, that I was going to start doing what I wanted to do with my life."

She told Jim, "I'm going after a good university job." She did, and she got it.

Six months later Jim was offered an administrative job for a textile firm in Wisconsin. He told Anna, "It's so good, I can't refuse."

So they talked. And they decided that neither of them should have to give up the work they most wanted to do.

Their commuting marriage began.

For the next six years the children stayed with Anna in Urbana, and Jim drove home on weekends. A year after the Wisconsin job came through, Jim left the company, this time to take an even better position with a land development company in Florida. It meant more money. The commuting was now done on airplanes, with Jim flying home every other weekend; once in a while, Anna would fly to Florida. And once every three months, all the children would go, too.

Anna lived the life of a single parent, fixing school

lunches at midnight and juggling schedules, but she loved it. She loved her work and as time went on she savored her independence and privacy.

Jim moved into a glossy apartment building with a shiny blue pool, and on Saturdays he would sit out on a deck chair and talk with stewardesses again. He valued his privacy, too.

Everybody, naturally, figured a divorce would follow.

"That made me lonely," says Anna. "We were going through some tough times, and it would have been nice if somebody had understood."

"It was toughest on you," says Jim.

They are silent for a moment.

"It just seemed to me that what had to be done, had to be done," says Jim. "If I try to figure what it is that has made our marriage work thus far, I think partly it's because we've let each other follow individual professional needs."

He folds his hands in back of his head. "Anna's never done anything to restrict me," he says. "She's always encouraged me to do what I wanted to do, and that matters very much. I think I've done the same for her."

He waits for a fraction of a second. She nods.

"What the hell else do you do?" he says. "For us, the commuting arrangement was right."

But it certainly disrupted their friendships.

"That's been one of the problems," says Jim. "I don't know what's going to happen now, but I imagine we'll do some socializing together." He thinks a moment and adds, "In one way, it isn't deeply important to me. I'm not the type of person who develops any quantity of friends. I guess

I'm rather a selfish person, but I tend not to worry about it too much. Apparently the way I live my life is humane enough so I don't alienate too many people." His smile is wry and brief. "But I do what I want to do, and I manage to have a few close friends."

He turns to Anna. "I consider Marie a close friend," he says.

"But she is my friend," says Anna.

Jim shrugs. "That's okay. She's my friend, independent of you. You know when I was here, and you were back in Iowa, I saw Marie quite a lot. I probably saw Marie more than I saw John."

Anna thinks about this for a moment, and then says slowly, "I think couples having couples as friends is really kind of phony. It's true, we don't have many mutual friends. Most of the people I see are people I work with, and when you get together as couples, it's not friendship. It's just what everybody who's married does on Friday and Saturday nights. I doubt if we'll ever have many mutual friends."

Jim obviously agrees. "I can't imagine the type of friend-ships that you see on television—people bowling once a week, going on picnics every other Saturday." He shakes his head. "I can't imagine seeing anybody on that constant a basis. In fact, I can't imagine anyone I'd want around that much."

"I can imagine it more than you can," says Anna.

"Sure," Jim says. "A woman doesn't get invited to as many places when she's alone. And yet there's nothing so strange about a guy in Miami without his wife."

The memory of Anna's face at the red plastic restaurant,

still and sad, came back to me as she said, "I want to be in love again, the way it's been before. Sure," she teases. "All those single women."

"I knew two or three of my neighbors, and the rest were just kind of nodding acquaintances," Jim says. "I got to know more people when Anna would visit." He turns to his wife. "You're more outgoing than I am," he says gently. "With you there, people found it easier to talk to me instead of asking each other, 'Who the hell is the guy we see sitting around the pool on weekends?'"

Mention of the pool brings a smile to Anna's face. "Hah, I had the kids all the time, and you know how that is. I'd leave the house at eight in the morning and get home at seven at night, and the only thing I did on weekends was clean up the house and take care of the kids."

The barbing is light. They raise their wineglasses in a brief, tacitly understood toast.

"There were many good things about being alone," says Anna quietly. "I loved coming home from work and putting the kids to bed and drawing the shades and realizing I could do what I wanted. Sometimes it was really gorgeous."

"Part of me, an important part, didn't like it at all," says Jim. "But I would never have wanted Anna to do something she didn't want to do."

Does he see himself as a liberated husband?

Jim shakes his head impatiently. "It isn't women's lib. It's Anna who affected me, who changed my attitudes. Women's lib came after. When Anna's job began shaping up I thought, Would I want to be kept from doing these things? And I thought, Hell, no, I wouldn't. I decided this family-housekeeping thing for women was a crock of shit. Nobody

134

with any—" He pauses. "I shouldn't say nobody with any sense wouldn't want to do it all the time, but nobody like me—and Anna's like me."

The brief ensuing silence is warm.

"If you were the kind of guy who had demanded every bit of me, I probably would have divorced you, I guess. Who knows? But I can't imagine living with that kind of person." Anna pauses. "You are good for me and I am good for you."

So commuting, then, was a mixed bag. Jim and Anna are not exceptionally "modern" people, and the avant-garde label slapped on them for their marital life style didn't make them very comfortable, although Anna is more at ease with change than Jim is.

Jim leans forward. "I want to talk about this a little," he says. "I want to explain how I look at life." He takes a deep breath. "I don't trust people who hold strong opinions very much," he says. "I think things change so rapidly that people find it easier to form instant prejudices instead of seasoned judgments. I'm a pragmatic person, and I can adjust to what is going on, but I don't have strong beliefs or values. That makes it easier to change them when you have to." He reflects. "I really don't feel very strongly about much of anything."

Anna nods her acceptance and adds, "I don't know if it's because things change so quickly, or because I'm getting older, but as we talk now I realize the only thing I ever really wanted to do was train myself to adjust. I don't know whether I'm preparing for nuclear war or the descent of some glacier, but I always expect disaster to come at some point. I've never planned for more than three or four years at most. I think, in a way, this is what we've been raising our children to think, too."

"We've kept some pretty traditional things going," objects Jim. "We're the authorities in this family, and I think that's healthy. The kids have to know there's always someone who's going to tell them what to do, and that there are things all of us have to do, whether we like it or not."

Anna shakes her head impatiently. "Oh, Jim, we don't know yet. Our kids are still younger than those of most people our ages. Remember Joan Biggs the other night telling us about how her son stood at the refrigerator and yelled, 'Fuck you, Mother'? I can't imagine that happening. But it might."

Jim thinks about that. Then he shakes his head. "Kids," he says.

Yes. Kids.

Says Jim, "If someone were to say to me today, 'What was the major mistake you made in your marriage?' I would say, 'Having children.' "

Says Anna, "I don't feel that way. If anybody asked me what the happiest times of my life have been, I would say, 'The time in the hospital after the birth of each child.' Nothing has been so completing, so joyous for me."

They say these things calmly to each other. It is a basic example of their differences. And Jim, as he points out, is not saying he does not love his children. With his own brand of flat-out honesty, he expands, "I think having children detracted from our relationship with each other. Anna and I have always enjoyed being together when we want to be, as much as we enjoy being alone when we want to be. But when the kids came in, they disrupted all this."

Anna thinks for a moment. "I have just begun to fully enjoy them as people," she offers.

"Well, I have too," amends Jim. "But still, I wish we had more of our lives to ourselves."

"I know." Anna sighs. "It's not so good for our sex life either."

"Lousy, I'd say," says Jim.

They share a momentary grumpy silence.

Anna perks up first. "We've been lucky, though," she says. "We've always agreed that we want to raise our children as independent people, and that's been very important."

Jim nods his head. "It sure is. And it includes pushing them into things, getting them out of the family world. And I think that's just fine. The more independent they are, the better off they are."

"I don't quite know how to put it," says Anna, "but we're a family of five people all doing their own thing. The family is where we come back to, where we get our wounds bandaged, where we help each other out." She pauses. "And that gift of independence encompasses me, too. I can't understand women who don't realize they need it as much as their kids."

Surely one of the most difficult adjustments of coming back together again is sharing authority in the home. Is Anna jealous of losing her role as the primary power figure?

"Sure, sometimes," she says. "But it isn't that important." She says this too quickly.

"Let's talk about money," suggests Jim.

Anna runs her hand quickly across her forehead. "That's been a real problem for us. It has caused our biggest arguments." She stops there, turns slightly in her chair toward Jim, and waits.

Jim moves uneasily. "Well, the truth is, whenever we've had some money, I've invested it very badly," he says. "It's only recently I've begun to realize you've got to save." He shakes his head in self-exasperation and continues, "I look back and I'm amazed at how stupid I've been. Anna and I inherited some money from my mother that could have helped us out, but I blew the whole damn thing on bad investments."

Anna consoles, obliquely. "I think the fact that I'm more oriented to saving and you are more oriented to spending was out of our control. We're simply carrying on the way our two mothers handled money."

"No, Anna, I lost all we had. Which wasn't much. I figured all you had to do was buy stock and it would automatically go up, if the company didn't go out of business."

"I think it was just your attitude that things would continue to get better and better."

"Wouldn't you say now, that I'm more of a financial pessimist than I was?" asks Jim. Anna nods, but he continues, offering proof. "I keep putting articles on your desk that say, 'Hey, look at the perils of Social Security; look at the federal debt; and look at the money the government's borrowing . . .'"

Anna smiles and says, "Yeah, but you're the one who talks, and I'm the one who saves. I'm the one squirreling away the pennies and that's always been our pattern. Jim always used to ask my advice before investing and I'd say, 'No, I don't think we should,' and he'd do it anyway. So then we had a period when we didn't dare talk about money. I was very, very angry." She looks across at her husband. "I don't know what Jim was feeling."

Jim shrugs his shoulders and says, "My feeling was, why talk about it? She had her opinion, and I had mine, so why talk about it? I'm not a kid. There was just no point in talking about it."

"I saved up more in my first three years of working than we did in fifteen years of marriage," Anna says with a particular edge to her voice.

How did that affect Jim?

Anna sighs. "I didn't tell him for a long time. Finally we talked."

"She's got savings now," Jim says lightly, "that I'm sure I don't know about."

"It was my way of getting back," Anna says calmly. "The last time we talked about it I said I was mad, and he said he knew I was and understood why, and now I feel good. My problem was I had been sitting for years worrying about saving money for the children's education and I didn't have the earning power. I was just the little wife saving money."

"Year after year I kept saying, we'll have it made," says Jim.

"Oh, I guess a lot of people feel that way," answers Anna.

"I guess this has been the most critical problem of all in our marriage," says Jim. "I can't recall being so resentful or angry about anything."

"It's much better now," says Anna.

There was silence again.

"We're loners," Anna says finally. "And we need privacy from each other—privacies in friendships, privacy in time. And I need"—with a glance toward Jim—"my own bank account. We need time together too. And a tough thing has been when my work blows a trip we've planned."

"That happens enough on both sides that we've kind of learned to live with it," says Jim. "When my work has meant canceling out on some of our plans, I feel very guilty even though there isn't a hell of a lot I can do about it. When it happens with Anna, I don't like it, but I accept it. I take the view that it's just one of those things that are beyond our control."

Neither Jim nor Anna is quite as sanguine as this sounds about the inroads on their time together. And for each of them, a tipping point was reached.

Anna remembers particularly one nightmare evening at a summer party. Jim was due in from Florida for the weekend, but at the last moment bad weather canceled his plans. So Anna went alone to the party. Friends nodded and smiled and chatted, and it was quite a while before she realized something devastating. "No one, absolutely no one, brought up Jim's name. They knew he was supposed to be there. But no one said, 'Well, how come Jim couldn't make it?' They were being polite. My God, everybody was avoiding mentioning his name completely. It was almost as if he were dead." That incident shook her deeply. It wasn't quite so dramatic for Jim, but the tipping point was just as real.

"My work began to get me down," he says. "I thought, What is everything *for*? To work like hell and sit around a pool by myself every other weekend? What was it all *for*?"

Resentments were growing. Independence was beginning to consume.

"We got to the point where we were giving so little to each other that we were in danger of walking off in opposite directions," says Anna. "We got more and more preoccupied with our separate lives. We just came together and went away and came back and went away again."

"If there had been a third party . . ." says Jim.

"I think we went out of our way to be decent to each other on that," says Anna.

"Once when I was alone in that damn apartment," says Jim slowly, "I figured there were about two hundred and fifty thousand women on the globe that I could be happily married to. But I didn't feel like going looking. Anna and I shared too many things." He looks quizzically at his wife. "I frankly think if there were a third party, it would be precipitated by Anna looking for a change or a challenge or excitement. I know what I've got, and I'm happy with it. I'm kind of slow-moving."

Anna looks toward the floor, and then up. "Why do people break up their marriages because they can't agree on basic things?" she asks. "Why do you have to agree on things? Why do you have to agree on politics? We don't. Or religion? The only thing you have to agree on is how you run your own lives, and your marriage."

"It never occurred to me to think about the number of things we disagree on," says Jim.

Anna smiles. "Fortunately," she says.

Jim quit his job and eventually decided to go into business for himself.

"Anna encouraged me," he says.

"I had the ability to carry us financially," she says.

"I was making about forty thousand dollars, and she was pulling in twenty-five thousand," says Jim. "I never would have had the opportunity to walk away from that place and take a little time deciding what to do next, if I hadn't had a working wife."

At that point Jim was deeply dissatisfied with the direction of his career; he felt he was spending his life working for other people when what he really wanted to do was work for himself. Half-heartedly, he began applying for jobs at companies where he felt he would have the best chance to gain autonomy. The job he was offered, over which he agonized, was in New York.

"Then one day sitting around here, it occurred to me—why the hell was I doing this?" He looks at Anna. "Why the hell were we just letting it happen? Why couldn't I find something in Urbana?"

Again Jim and Anna talked. And again they reset the pattern of their lives.

"That's when I got interested in a restaurant franchise business here a friend told me about. I talked to the guy managing the place, and made up my mind overnight."

Jim smiles, his warmest smile of the evening, and leans forward in his chair, his chin high. "You know, I just did it!"

Clearly, these two people, this husband and this wife, see the decision to live together again full time, under one roof, in one town, as the most important of their married lives.

"I wanted him home. I really wanted him home," says Anna, and there is remembered loneliness in her voice.

"We both wanted that," says Jim. "But being apart wasn't all that bad. In fact, a lot of the crap that comes up now never came up then. I never felt our marriage was in jeopardy, because we worked harder at making the time we spent together decent." He draws a deep breath and adds, "I was more concerned about my ability to live full time with the kids."

The adjustments began, and they were feared because neither Jim nor Anna quite knew what was necessary. They were two people who knew each very well, who shared memories of tenderness and pain, who shared a long history, and yet they had not shared a tube of toothpaste in six years. Would giving up critical portions of their lives alone destroy what they wanted to share together?

"I woke up in the middle of the night a day or two after Jim came home for good," says Anna. "We'd gotten to bed late or something, and having him there disrupted my ordinary rhythms, I guess. I woke up and sat up and looked across at him sleeping on the other side of the bed. And I broke into a cold sweat, and I thought, My God, what's going to happen? This will never work. I was scared to death."

And so was Jim. "I was driving with a friend downtown, telling him about moving back home, and I said, 'The only trouble with our marriage is that when we get back together on a full-time basis, it will be a shock for us both.' And then I knew I was scared." Now they mutually take the pulse of their marriage.

"It's gone pretty smoothly," says Anna. "We're trying to be thoughtful with each other when our ways of doing things are different."

"We've got less money for now," says Jim. "It'll be a while before the restaurant starts getting profitable. And I'm touchy with the kids."

"Jim, they're so glad you're home, they don't mind."

Jim nods, plainly appreciating the reassurance.

"I wasn't sure for a long, long time," Anna says slowly. "But I know now how much I want you and our marriage. Forty percent of me is you."

Jim laughs. "If sixty percent of you were me, my love, we'd both be in deep trouble."

"If you had demanded that much, we'd have been divorced long ago," she retorts.

"I wonder what makes our marriage work?" Jim's question is sudden, curious.

Anna shakes her head. She wants to think about that.

"From my point of view," says Jim, "I don't have an overwhelming dependence on you, and I think that goes both ways. I think our relationship has gotten better over the years. You know, I guess for most of us when we get married, we romanticize things. We figure we want total involvement and total dependence. That could be great, I suppose. But I think trying to live that way is more strain than ninety-nine percent of people can cope with."

Anna nods her head vigorously.

And what, I ask, is irreplaceable in this marriage?

"Nothing," Anna responds promptly.

"Oh, sure there is, but it's hard to put my finger on," says Jim. "It's that indefinable something that I have in the fun of being with Anna and doing things with Anna. I don't know what the hell it is but we've always just had a good time being together."

Anna remembers something, and laughs. "Jim, remember last Sunday, that disastrous picnic where everything went wrong?"

"I forgot the grill," Jim says.

"And I forgot the buns," says Anna. "So we had raw hamburgers and potato chips and the sillier it got, the funnier it got."

Jim leans forward in his chair. "We have good times, don't we?"

Anna nods.

"I don't know," says Jim. "No matter what the situation is, it's always been easy for me to do anything with Anna. I don't know why. But that's been the magic of the thing."

Anna says, "I'll tell you what's irreplaceable. Having experienced with you over fifteen critical years of my life. There's so much we've shared. It's just there as part of him and part of me, and I don't think you ever get rid of that."

Is this, then, in essence, their descriptions of what love is in their relationship?

"I would guess that," says Jim.

And Anna says the same.

The wine is almost gone. The room has turned chilly, and we prepare to end the evening. Anna starts to collect the glasses and Jim looks at his watch in mock horror: it is almost three o'clock. Then Anna says, "I didn't know how lovely it would be to have someone to come home to again. Remember how high I was, Jim, that first week you were back?"

"Yeah, I remember. You were up on a cloud, even though the business thing wasn't settled, and I didn't know what I was going to do for sure."

She shrugs. "Oh well, security. Doesn't mean that much. We make our own."

"That's right, babe. And I guess we always will."

I stay two days with Anna and Jim, and it is clear they are working hard—perhaps too hard. The home could use more laughter, but it is not lacking in tenderness. These are two people clearly doing what they want to do. But they have stage fright.

By most modern definitions, Jim and Anna come across as experimenters daring enough to dabble with the traditional and remake the rules. But they aren't really innovators at heart, and they know it. Their marital values are conservative, which makes the choices and risks they took so interesting. They didn't live apart because they couldn't stand each other. And they didn't come back together again out of fear. They experimented, I believe, because they are both more able to live with uncertainty and risk than most people.

They describe themselves as loners, and it seems to be true. But because it is a trait they share, it is, in a curious way, one of their strongest bonds. They also share remarkably similar backgrounds. They married knowing accurately the sharp taste of each other's childhood loneliness, although Jim was clearly more impoverished emotionally because of a demanding mother who gave little nurturing.

I suspect Jim was the less self-reliant of the two in the commuting years. There is a fragile quality to this person who continually declares his emotional invincibility. My mental image of Jim lounging by a Florida apartment-house pool is that of a lonely man, and his declarations of neutrality on most of life's issues do not ring true.

Anna, like many other women of her generation, came late to the pleasures of professional achievement. The thrill of it all is still new. At midlife, many men feel they are running down. They are aware of the doors now forever closed to them, and they don't see many left to open. They become depressed, wondering what it is all for. At the same time, their wives are moving out of the home, going to school or work, viewing midlife as the time when opportunities open up, not close down.

Jim is not as enthusiastic about work as Anna. And he has done the major share of accommodating to life style in the marriage. But Anna's good salary has made it possible for Jim, at the age of forty-one, to take on the risks of starting a new career—one example of what interdependence in marriage can mean. Yet it has caused problems. There is not as much money as there was before, and Jim is sensitive to the fact that he made bad financial investments. I did not sense great tension about money, but as a continuing theme of the marriage, it is there.

The balance? Jim's need for Anna is greater than her need for him in terms of central emotional investments; hers laps over more to the children and to her work.

Jim's negativism about the children is partly because, as he said, he sees them as intruders between himself and Anna. It is also partly connected to his strong desire for peace and quiet. The children exist. They are there, with their snakes and model planes and report cards and all the demands that make any parent, at times, want to take a walk. Permanently. I also think he is wary of how securely he can forge the emotional bond between himself and his children because of his own failure with his mother.

But it is Anna's response that offers a reasonable perspective: if this man she loves did not love the children, there would be more observable anger and tension. Whatever the reasons for his feelings, she accepts.

The final afternoon, Anna drove me back to the airport. We talked peacefully of unimportant things, and we both agreed it had been a good and a warm weekend. As she pulled the car into the airport parking lot, a shadow fell across her face and she turned to me. "We told you a lot," she said quietly, "but nobody can let anyone in totally. You understand that, don't you?"

There is a postscript to the story of the Lowells which I add now, many months after that goodbye. I debated first about removing the story of Anna and Jim from this book, but I decided that was not only a phony way of tidying up the truth, it was also a denial of the fact that they did indeed work at their marriage, and that it mattered to them both. Its end was cruel, but that end is part of their reality. And so, this postscript. One cold winter morning Anna awoke to find Jim gone from their bed. She walked downstairs and into the kitchen which connects with the garage. Only then did she hear the car motor running. Anna remembers the sound of her own voice screaming as she threw open the garage door and saw, through the haze of monoxide fumes, Jim's body slumped across the front seat.

Weeks later, we talked. Her face pale, her swollen eyes

hidden behind sunglasses, Anna tried as best as she could to find reasons for Jim's suicide: the restaurant business had not moved ahead very well, and Jim had begun working longer and longer hours. Twice they had planned a vacation together; twice he had backed out at the last moment, unable to pull himself away from his work. The second time, angry, Anna announced she was going without him, and so she did, holding his ticket until the last moment, hoping he would change his mind.

Her decision to go alone drew a heavy line under a growing problem in the mariage: the gap between the vitality of his life outside the marriage and the vitality of Anna's. That line was drawn deeper upon her return. "I told him the truth," she whispered. "I had a wonderful time by myself."

They talked a long time that evening of her return. They talked of separating. They talked almost all night, and the next day there was little left to say. His death came two days later.

What happened to these people? I have looked back through my many notes made over that weekend and tried to piece together some reasons. But the connecting tissue remains a series of unanswerable questions, for in the end, really, no one will ever know precisely why Jim chose to take his own life.

But I think a process of destruction had been under way for a long time. Jim was faced with career changes he couldn't handle, and with the vitality of a wife not only able to financially support them both but capable of achieving emotional satisfaction without him as well. Jim learned long ago to be careful with his emotions.

Tracing the line of bitterness and coldness back to a

prime source is not hard—Jim's relationship with his mother. A man's feelings about his mother are enormously important in shaping his future relationships with women. I think it's so important that it's one of the first questions I ask when in the process of getting to know a man. Did he like his mother? Love her? Respect her?

One day last summer I sat at a veranda table outside the gleaming white walls of the Los Angeles County Museum with a man I had come to know fairly well, listening to a story that still appalls me. One afternoon he had picked up the phone and called his parents, who lived a thousand miles away. After a few moments of talk with his mother, he asked, "How's Dad?" There was a brief pause, then: "Not too good, son." "What's the matter?" he asked. Again, a pause. "Well, he had a heart attack last week." "My God," said my friend, "why didn't you let me know?" "Well, son, last Sunday was Father's Day, and I thought you would call . . ."

My friend hung up the phone and took the next plane home. His father died shortly thereafter.

Now, I can think of no better example of what I call the Bitch Mother, for this woman had done an ultimate guilt number on her son. After hearing his story, I wasn't at all surprised to learn of his smashed marriage and other failed relationships, for how could he ever trust and love a woman with that model?

The Bitch Mother is not wholly villain; she is usually a woman who demands love by inflicting guilt because she has no confidence in her essential worth. She sees herself as powerless in the general scheme of life, and yet often exerts great power within her family—in the manipulative ways that have come to be defined as traditionally female—to the detriment of the lives of men and the reputations of women. Sometimes when the Bitch Mother's son has grown, he marries "her" because he sees no other game in town. Bitch Mother becomes Bitch Wife. Other times he marries a woman not at all like his mother, but he never really knows because he never allows her emotionally close enough to find out.

And still other times he seems to break free, marrying for better reasons, then investing all emotional needs in that one person.

What happens when such a man then discovers his wife can get along without him? Often nothing less than destruction of the male ego, according to sociologist Jesse Bernard. This is what happened to Jim.

Take just the simple fact that Anna was financially independent. How does a man retain his maleness in such a situation? What remains of his traditional male role? He can't haul home the family dinner on his back after a day's hunt. Yet if he can't at least bring in the family paycheck, what is his essential importance?

Some kind of answers for these questions is needed in a society where twenty million wives work at paying jobs outside the home. We're really talking about nothing less than changing the social construct of maleness. Is it possible?

Norman M. Lobsenz concluded after a survey for *Redbook* magazine that most husbands harbor deeply ambivalent feelings about working wives. Oh, sure, it's great having the extra income coming into the family coffers. And they feel lucky not to have neurotic, complaining stay-at-home wives who want the world delivered daily on a silver platter by their husbands. On the other hand, a woman who makes her own income automatically carries just a bit more clout. If it's her money being spent too, then maybe she won't go along with that splurge on a new BMW. Maybe she will flatly and calmly say "No." Then what happens to the traditional balancing of marital power in the home? Is the husband able to retool; to accept her thumbs-down position as equally important as his own feelings?

And there's more than a power struggle involved. For although many men don't care to admit it, they worry about their wives having affairs, and with good reason. A recent national survey showed that 47 out of every 100 working wives have had extramarital affairs, compared with only 27 out of 100 nonworking wives. It's more than succumbing to increased opportunity, for if there's already trouble in the marriage, an affair may be what propelled the wife out of the home and into a job. And I doubt if any sensible man would try to slam the front door shut on his wife, in the "keep her barefoot and pregnant" philosophy of exerting male control. But they are uneasy. (Another recent study at the University of California indicates the sharpest recent increase in divorces has occurred in marriages where the wives did not work outside the home. A comforting counterpoint?)

The complications of all of this weave together and wind around confusingly, among money, power, sex—and something more. First, what about the situation where the wife earns more money than the husband? Not only did that happen with the Lowells, but Jim had to deal with the fact that Anna's money was paying for everything, finally. When the differences in husband-wife incomes are quite spectacular, and reporters go questioning with their notebooks and pencils, men tend to respond with more serenity, I suspect, than they actually feel. "It's no big deal," said a Midwestern HEW official married to a glamorous television personality whose annual income topped his by thousands of very heavy dollars. "I'm delighted," he proclaimed with a grin. "It just means more money for the family unit."

I talked with a Northwestern University professor and got a more honest answer. "I'm proud of my wife's success in her work," he said. "But it takes her into contact with far more people than my job does. That means she's developing more interests and a wider range of friends than I am. She'll end up being more interesting to other people than I will be." He paused. "I'm jealous of that. And it scares me."

This man's honest expression of his feelings helped me to understand Jim Lowell a little better. How can one partner in a marriage, no matter how sensitive, understand the mixture of bravado and bitterness the other must hide, when convinced he or she lives under a declining star? How could Jim express jealousy of Anna's superior energies, her life force, without drawing too achingly the contrasts with his own deficiencies? Not easily. In our culture the man must be strong. He must keep all the child within him, not cry out in the dark. Better for him to shatter like glass than ooze from the core.

It's a cultural cruelty, a really terrible one, I thought one night, at a point where I was unable to write one more word about Jim Lowell. All that carefulness, all that pridefulness.

Jim's fears affected everything. During the commuting part of their marriage, the comfortable and satisfying sex he and Anna had enjoyed dwindled to nothing. It wasn't the scheduling so much; it was the emotional carefulness, the apprehension that affected them both. They were elaborately careful not to question each other on what happened when they were apart. Looking back now, Anna believes Jim was terrified he would lose her. "I never felt the same terror," she said. She didn't feel it, she couldn't understand it. But she reacted to it. And the well of mutual support and encouragement began to run dry.

Was it the commuting that destroyed this marriage and this man? Many couples are experimenting with its uncertainties. They are trying to resolve conflicts, not create them. Do they have a chance, or will this be one more marital experiment of the seventies to go down the drain, sucking numerous marriages with it? My own experience doesn't offer a positive contrast. I worked for a year and a half in Chicago, eighty miles away from my family, commuting home on weekends. It was a painful, lonely time. And as it turned out, it was a marital risk that didn't work. But it didn't cause my eventual divorce, it just underscored many of the reasons why it was inevitable.

Yet there are a number of couples who do carry it off, although I haven't found any who advise commuting for a long period of time. "I'd say two years at the outside," said one husband who taught in Indiana, commuting to Wisconsin each weekend. "Then you've got to do something else. Otherwise you grow too far apart."

I know one couple from a small town in Oregon who embarked on a venture similar to my own and to that of the Lowells. Their marriage was strained; differences were pulling at them. It wasn't just a practical solution for conflicting careers, it was also a testing time. For two years, she worked in a hospital in Cleveland, returning home only at Christmas and for parts of the summer. One child lived with him, and one with her.

She called me one winter afternoon, which surprised me, for we hadn't seen each other in ten years. When we met for dinner, I was struck by the absence of a special ebullience I remember so well. Susan had always been a woman who bounced out of a chair, whose hair swung when she laughed, who hugged her friends with a special exuberance that had a way of infecting anyone lucky enough to be around. Gone. In its place was a carefully controlled smile, measured movements, even carefully combed and lacquered hair.

She described many of the same problems and uncertainties Anna Lowell had talked about. She acknowledged a long affair and questioned coolly whether she still loved her husband. She smoked two packs of cigarettes during dinner. I wondered for the hundredth time why I was writing a book on working marriages.

And then she said, "I don't know fully what it is that holds us together, but deep down it is a friendship that never seems to end. Always, we know we would somehow be there for each other." She paused, for just a moment, less certain, and all the hard lines that traced her seemed softer. "It's more than that, or different from that. I don't know, I really don't know what will happen to us."

A few weeks later I received a short letter from her husband. He said Susan had told him of our meeting, and he wanted to say hello once again himself, across those ten years. "You know something now of our situation," he wrote. "We're trying. But nothing much is very sure in this world. Please wish us well."

I folded up that note, thinking of Andy, that quiet, bespectacled man who had written it, and I realized how much I wished them well. I did, and I do. And given what has happened since, I think they are making it.

Susan gave up her job. She packed her bags, said goodbye to the particular package of life she had fashioned for herself alone, and went back to Oregon. It was no career sacrifice. She found a good job there. She and her husband gathered their kids and their sleeping bags and went off into the Oregon mountains for two months. Some things have begun to heal; others are just patched over. But they seem to have much more going for them than Jim and Anna had. Andy's job is more stable; more important, so is his ego.

"How," cried Anna, that last painful afternoon in the restaurant, "could I have known Jim for so many years, lived with him, shared all we shared, and never, never have dreamed he was capable of killing himself?"

For her, that is the hardest of the unanswerable questions.

the sensualist...
and her husband

Laurie and Bob

Laurie Kincaid gave up wearing bras somewhere back in the early seventies. She's casual about her clothes, preferring tee shirts and wrap skirts to anything else. Her style of dress makes for an interesting contrast, for with her thin, fine-boned face, her quiet voice and outward reserve, she looks like a candidate for president of the League of Women Voters. She seems, at one and the same time, outwardly, a woman of the seventies and a woman of the fifties.

The early molding of a good Catholic convent-educated girl doesn't rub off easily. Laurie lived the whole scene: twelve years of convent school with morning mass and the Angelus at noon and rosaries with her family at night. Kindly aunts would smile and pat her cheek and tell her she would make a good nun. Laurie didn't want that. She dreamed of being rich. She bought her lipsticks from Woolworth's and her sweaters from Sears, and she often wished that her father wasn't just a plumber.

Then one afternoon Laurie came home from school and found a letter of acceptance plus a promise of a scholarship from the Eastern women's college she hungered for. She was elated. Without that money, it would have meant the state college in Montana.

College meant meeting new people, confronting new ideas. And very quickly it meant dumping mass and confession and all the accouterments of Catholicism.

"My father was hurt," she says. "He wrote me a letter and said I was doing it for snob reasons, and I wrote back and told him no, that wasn't true. I just didn't believe any longer. I had met people I respected who sort of mocked my unthinking responses to catechism questions, and when I began thinking about it, I didn't believe."

She decided giving up religion was part of growing up and it took a long time before she and her father were able to talk about it again.

Laurie was bright and curious and eager, and she did well in school. When the time came to celebrate her twenty-first birthday, she had a wealthy boyfriend whose legal coming of age happened to be on the same day. For him, the day meant a substantial inheritance. For Laurie, it meant a memorable sexual initiation.

"Fantastic," she remembers with relish. "We went to a fancy hotel and ordered a fabulous supper and we crawled into bed together and it was great. The only thing that disappointed me was that I didn't bleed all over the sheets. I had kind of expected that. It's the way it always happened in books. But there wasn't even enough blood to make a good-sized spot."

Months later, Laurie met Bob. His family was socially prominent and they had money, but that, she had already found out, wasn't the hardest combination in the world to find. More than by money or status, Laurie was drawn to this man by his quiet stability. Already she sensed she would need it.

Her parents were pleased. From their savings and Laurie's they scraped together enough money for an expensive marital launching. Laurie walked down the aisle in a long white gown and she had five bridesmaids and a hotel reception and everybody got drunk on medium-good champagne.

When the wedding was over, both Laurie and her parents were broke, but it had been done right, and Bob's parents had no reason to feel shamed.

Laurie, the daughter of a small-town plumber, had married a young doctor with good connections and a great future.

"I figured that was it," she says. "My future from then on was nicely mapped out. I'd work a little while at something and then I'd get pregnant and we would raise our family." She adds reflectively, "The thing that strikes me more than anything else, is that young people I know now who are dating are obviously trying to communicate their feelings and their expectations. In no way, shape, or form were those reasonable topics of conversation then. It simply didn't occur to us to talk about them very much. We figured you got married and you lived happily ever after, and that was that."

That was fifteen years ago. Since then, there have been two distinct periods of the Kincaid marriage: the first ten years, when Laurie had eleven extramarital affairs and no children; and the last five, when she had two children—and no affairs.

Laurie apologizes instantly for the disarray of her home as we walk in the front door, explaining, "I've always hated housework totally, but with working and all, it's worse now."

The air is sticky hot, and she has pulled her dark, gray-streaked hair back into a tight bun, wrapping a lavender chiffon scarf around it, letting the ends trail loose. On someone else, it would look kitschy. On Laurie, it becomes Instant Class.

"I'm glad we got here before Bob," she says. "It's probably best to fill you in on the sex stuff before he gets home. It'll be a little easier on him."

She stands in the kitchen doorway, gazing at the ironing board set up by the sink still filled with morning dishes. Cereal bowls with dried Wheaties flakes are stacked on top of wine glasses. She pulls jars of jam and peanut butter out of the cupboard and starts preparing sandwiches on the ironing board.

How come she does this with grace? I don't know, but she does. How come it doesn't look slovenly? I don't know, but it doesn't.

"You can see I need household help," she says calmly. "Right now that would make things easier for us. The children are still so little it's impossible to keep their messes tidied up when I'm gone most of the day." She finishes her job, puts away the jars. "I know most women complain their husbands don't help much around the house," she says. "It doesn't work that way here. Bob is great about helping, particularly when company's coming. But his schedule—" She shakes her head and smiles. "You know doctors."

Bob works long hours in the local hospital of this small North Carolina town where he and Laurie have lived now for four years. For a few years, Laurie worked part time on various jobs, more for something to do than for the money. But she is a talented woman, and her administrative abilities caught the attention of a large corporation located just outside their town. She works for them now, with increasing responsibilities. She likes it, but this, too, sits lightly. "I've never really developed much of a commitment to a career," she says. "I've never felt my ego was all that involved, where I couldn't drop a job and do things I wanted to do with Bob."

Bob is also inclined to keep some distance between himself and his work, not in the sense of lessened interest, but in the sense of not allowing it to anchor him. He isn't ready for that yet. He isn't ready to set up a small-town practice, resigning himself to seeing the same people day after day over the years. He has worked on a cruising hospital ship. He spent two years as a resident in an English hospital. He hopes to pick up and go again in a few years, perhaps to Austria, a country he loves. Laurie intends to stay uncommitted enough to her work to be able to go with him.

The sandwiches are served. Laurie takes two bottles of beer out of the refrigerator, and we sit down to eat.

"Our first year of marriage was murderous," she begins.

Bob chose to serve his internship at a teaching hospital in Pennsylvania. He lived the standard grueling existence of a young doctor, working long hours, leaving their small apartment early each morning, arriving home late each night, tumbling into bed exhausted, falling asleep instantly.

"Every morning the alarm would go off at five-fifteen," Laurie remembers. "For a while I tried to get up with him and have a cup of coffee, but he left at a quarter of six, and neither of us could talk that early anyway. The days were awful. Empty. Boring. I'd watch television at night, and at eleven o'clock Bob would stagger in the door." She smiles. "Every other Sunday he had an afternoon off. Weren't we lucky?"

Laurie met other bored doctors' wives, but she felt restless around them, unwilling to be a stoic. And because she was attractive and outgoing as well as bored, she soon began to meet men—with a look, a laugh exchanged in the elevator, a chat at the drugstore.

"I began an affair," she says. "It went on for quite a while, without Bob knowing. I felt kind of debased. It was my background and all." She speaks matter-of-factly, flatly, in a "pass the butter, please" style that is jarring at first. Later I understand Laurie does this to strip her sexual history of its drama, to make it less painful.

"When it was over, I thought we'd be all right. I felt great relief. Things did stabilize for a while, but Bob's routine didn't change. And then I met another man."

Anyone making book on the Kincaid marriage in the following six years would have bet heavily on an early divorce. There never were those early shining moments that older marrieds look back to nostalgically. There never would be. Bob did not stay blind to his wife's affairs, but he tried to ignore them, even to pretend they weren't happening. It was the way his mother had lived through thirty-five years with his father. It was the only thing he felt equipped to do.

Each affair whipped closer in to the heart of the marriage. Laurie finally reached the one which took on a classic self-redemptive twist. "I thought I loved him, and all of my wandering from man to man could end," she says. He was married too, and a strong part of their bond was exchanging constant complaints about spouses, but of course, it didn't appear that way at the time.

Laurie's lover urged her to leave Bob. He promised he would leave his wife and the two of them would be married.

"I thought this was the right thing to do," she says. She hurries past the details. "I told Bob . . . and left him. Then the other guy said, 'Gee, that's nice. But I can't really leave my wife.' I—how could I go back to Bob and say, 'Sorry, I changed my mind'?"

But she did. The way Laurie sees it now, getting dumped off the merry-go-round was the best thing that could have happened. Suddenly Bob did not look dull in his constancy. Suddenly she began realizing a little more what she felt for this man.

That was all very nice, of course, but "suddenly" isn't the way a marriage as tattered and torn as this one gets put back together again.

Laurie began seeing a psychiatrist.

"It was the smartest thing I ever did," she says, reverting to her pass-the-butter tone.

"I'm a born flirt. When I'm attracted to a man, I want him to see me as the best. And if part of that means being the best in a sexual way, that's okay. Or, I should say, it was."

There have been no other men for nine years, but not because Laurie is any less interested. It has been an essential compromise.

"I had to decide between being a flirt or staying married," she explains. "Sexual fidelity is not that big a thing to me—but it is to Bob, and therefore it has to be to me—if I want my husband."

She stops and looks at me closely. "Probably not many women tell you this kind of a story." I nod. It's true.

"I'll try to explain a little more," she continues. "I just don't think sex is that important. I've never had a first occasion with a man which mattered much. Either the guy thinks you're a whore, or he takes it too seriously, or you're nervous or can't perform or fumbling, and it's just disaster." She takes a deep breath. "So sleeping with different men isn't all that interesting. Now I don't see an affair as a betrayal. But I know the difference between then and now: I was less involved with Bob in all ways, and that was where the destruction took place. I was nagged by horrible guilt pangs and I kept Bob at a distance, and then I would do things to get back at him to justify my guilt. Is this making sense?"

Yes, this is making sense.

"I don't mean to have that all going one way," she says. "I think if Bob were unfaithful to me now, and it wasn't a woman who threatened me or my children or our marriage, it wouldn't bother me in the slightest."

Not even the tiniest pang of anger or jealousy?

Laurie hesitates for only a second. She shakes her head firmly. "No."

The sun has begun to dip toward the west, and Laurie suddenly looks at the kitchen clock. "Bob's late," she says, and then laughs. "Hope he didn't get cold feet about the interview." She clears the table, and goes to the telephone, dialing the hospital. "Sometimes in the mornings when he's in a hurry, he won't hear my reminders." She turns her attention to the phone. "Oh, he's almost through? Good . . . No, don't bother him." She hangs up and comes back to the table. "We've got another twenty minutes to ourselves," she says.

We open two more beers. She looks at me curiously, and says, "Do you ever find yourself not liking the people you interview?"

Yes, that happens. But not usually. When it does, I find it very difficult to write about them, I tell her.

She nods. "This has all been very tough on Bob," she says quietly. "We talked quite a while about whether or not we were ready to share things with you. But screwy as it may sound to some people, we have something good."

We both hear the car turning into the gravel driveway outside at the same instant. Laurie looks up, and smiles. "Here he is," she says.

The man who walks through the front door looks much younger than thirty-six at first glance. He is tall and thin, with the athletic good looks of a certain type you see often on California beaches. But you know you would never see him in such a setting. This is much too serious a person to loll amidst the pleasures of sun and sand. If you saw Bob Kincaid from across a room at a party, you would type him immediately as a doctor. Even without a white coat, he looks carefully starched and pressed. It isn't that he actually *is;* he just communicates a strong sense of internal order. His eyes are solemn and large. He looks first toward Laurie.

"Hey, you ought to hear what we've already got on tape," jokes Laurie.

He glances quickly at me. "I don't care what you've said," he answers. He walks into the kitchen, opens a beer, and joins us at the table.

There is a short and awkward silence.

"Where are you at?" he asks in his own version of pass-the-butter.

"I told Pat about my last affair," says Laurie. "And starting therapy."

He nods. "It was a tough time."

Bob wanted Laurie back when her romance fell through. He wasn't really sure why; he was just sure. But those next few months were almost unendurable. They would sit at dinner, alternately staring at each other and looking away, talking about what had happened to them and talking about things that mattered not at all.

Bob thought he could live with the realization that Laurie had wanted to end their marriage by leaving him for another man. He had absorbed the blow when it came, but he found living with the memory of it afterward was much harder.

They decided to separate. Bob left to spend a year on the hospital ship. Laurie continued her therapy. And in anybody's book, the odds for the two of them were way down.

"We began to write each other every day," says Bob. "Long, long letters. Every time I sat down to write, I felt there wasn't anybody who could measure up to Laurie—in any way."

Laurie nods gravely. "We had more to say to each other on paper in that year than at any time before in our marriage."

As the year wore on, their letters became longer. They began to share more honestly their feelings and values. And because they still had the protection of distance, the flash points—the hurts and angers—were diluted. As they look back on it now, they realize they both were learning to be vulnerable.

"Crazy word, isn't it?" says Bob. His smile is shy, a little worried. "Important, though."

For Laurie, the year of therapy was an all-important buffer zone. She talked out her attitudes toward men, sex, the Catholic Church and Bob's consuming work.

For Bob, that year meant some experimenting, too. He slept with different women, tried in his own, non-swinging way to build a buffer zone.

"All it did was convince me I loved my wife," he says.

When it was over, the Kincaids put aside their letters and their past, and started living their marriage once again.

"We figured it was time to start a family," says Bob.

Weren't they afraid of falling into a classic trap? Instead of cementing their marriage ties, having a child could exacerbate their differences and lock them in.

"No, we weren't," says Laurie. "We got back together in April, and by August we were pretty sure that things were going to work out for us, at least as well as anything does. So we decided to go ahead."

"Well, it was the reason to be married in the first place," says Bob.

"Hey, wait a minute—"

"What I mean is, it was one of the reasons to be married," Bob amends. "We weren't having a baby to hold us together. If we were going to do that, we would have done it during the first six years."

Motherhood suited Laurie. With her little girl, life began to develop a calm and substantive center. Within a year and a half Bob and Laurie decided to have a second child. They both found an easy bonding with their children and a deepening sense of family.

"We've been building things," says Bob. "You know, it becomes harder and harder to be separate, the more things you share. It's the way you define yourself . . ."

"I know I'm much better off married," says Laurie. "I don't think I'd be very happy if my life was a series of one-night stands—or six-month stands."

She waits for Bob to speak.

"So many things have become part of me that are part of Laurie. Big things and little things. We both love to cook. We play a lot with the children. I cherish them. I couldn't do without them."

Laurie squirms slightly in her chair. He, the outwardly calm, reserved doctor, is expressing emotion—emotionally. She, the outgoing, gregarious one, is clearly less comfortable with this. She puts the conversation back on a practical level. "We've worked out a good routine," she says. "I don't feel resentful of Bob's work any more."

"It isn't easy being a doctor and having a family," he says.

The alarm may go off at 5:15 A.M. some days, but not every day. Bob may work until 11 P.M., too, but definitely not every day.

Bob has made a concentrated effort to break the hammerlock of his consuming routine, which isn't easy for a man as engrossed in his work as he is. But he has no aspirations to rise in the administration of the hospital, and no overwhelming ambition to be first in his field.

So coming home on Saturday and taking the kids to the park playground is not a sacrifice. It is not reluctantly sandwiched in. "I'm learning to work less and talk more," Bob says with a small smile.

"It's not that you always succeed," Laurie reminds him quickly. "It's that I always know you are trying."

Bob thinks for a moment, and then says, "I like to think that you've done most of the changing."

"Oh, Bob, you changed a lot," she answers. "We talk together, much, much more than ever before."

"Yeah," he concedes. "It's still hard sometimes for me to recognize my feelings when I have them. That's where I've changed, I guess."

Silently the three of us consider the trade-offs made. I detect no smugness, no balancing off of who-makes-the-most-concessions-around-here, no phony generosity. Are there residual resentments? Of course.

"But we've come to a good accommodation," Bob says.

"Oh, we still have big differences," says Laurie.

Their attitudes toward money, for example.

"I *hate* bargaining in stores," says Laurie heatedly. "Bob loves to go around pricing things, different stereo sets or whatever, trying to get the best buy."

"That's because you hated being poor," he says.

She shrugs. "I want good things. Not junk."

"Laurie, you're basically a spendthrift."

She bridles slightly. "Well, things were easy for you."

"I know," answers Bob. "I guess I'm almost a penny pincher—because it's a challenge, I guess. It's a waste to throw something away, and when it comes to something like buying a car, I look through the ads for days." He glances at Laurie with a smile. "That bothers you."

"No, no," she says earnestly. "It doesn't bother me that *you* do it. I wouldn't do it because I'm too lazy, but what bothers me is to be along when you're bargaining." She turns to me and says, "When I used to go into a store as a child, I didn't want anyone to know I didn't have much money. I figured if I tried on a dress or a sweater that I thought was twelve dollars and it turned out to be twenty dollars, I'd have to walk away, but I'd never admit it was because of the price." Laurie seems suddenly aware of the intensity in her voice. She sits back, then says, "I actually have a very nice family."

"Yes, you do," Bob says.

"Even with the disagreement on the Church—" Laurie smiles. "My mother isn't Catholic, and it's made for some differences. My father always said we should thank God for our blessings, and my mother said we get where we are in life from our own hard work. Two sides of the coin."

"It's a good marriage," says Bob.

"Yes," answers Laurie. "I think it's gotten better for them as time has gone by. My father has never been terribly ambitious, and they've gotten by on very little money, but they've been happy." Her voice is tender. She harbors no resentment that her father didn't try to "get ahead" and he apparently has long since made his accommodation on Laurie's leaving the Church. "He's sort of given up on the Church anyhow," she says. "He still believes in God, but my two sisters and I all married non-Catholics, and the priests in our local parish were horrible about it."

"Things were different in my family," says Bob.

"Your *father*—" Laurie's voice is indignant. "He tried to stamp out any spontaneity that Bob ever had, always telling him to 'think of the consequences' before saying what he felt. What a rigid way to be brought up."

Bob is watching Laurie. "Well, that's changing," he says.

"You know what the nicest thing about my family is?" Laurie says suddenly to Bob. "They never cling. They leave us alone."

Laurie fiddles for a moment with the scarf around her hair, drawing her fingers through the chiffon, then bunching it in her fist. She has more to say about her family. "When I was in therapy, I had to try to figure out if I'd gotten screwed up as a child. And I don't think so. It's more that I was always angry at Bob and unable to bend my own pride to talk with him about things. In a way, that was losing face. So I got back with the affairs."

Bob's expression doesn't change. "It was the crowd we knew too," he says.

Laurie nods. "People were so rootless, and there was an awful lot of musical beds going on among our friends. It fascinated me. It was so interesting." She laughs. "I remember when I was a teenager, my mother was always reading these torrid historical novels, sitting there in the living room, shaking her head, saying, 'I know they make it up. People just don't live this way.' "

She pauses, glances at Bob, and says, "Then I discovered they sure did."

For a moment Laurie's delight with the excitement of it all surfaces. She makes no attempt to pretend it isn't there. Nor does Bob try to walk around it.

"Playing musical beds never appealed to me," he says. He smiles with just the faintest hint of apology in my direction, as if to erase a faintly self-righteous flavor to his answer. "I wasn't more moral about it," he says. "It just didn't appeal."

Their friendships now are much more settled. And they are almost all shared.

"We don't know many people who have been divorced in the last seven or eight years," says Bob. Some of the people they know work at the hospital, others at the corporation where Laurie is working.

"We never go to night clubs, and rarely even to parties," says Laurie. "Usually we have a few people over to dinner, or go to dinner at another couple's house. It's very pleasant."

"It suits us both," says Bob.

A problem looming is Laurie's work. "I've gotten really involved with it," she says. "And pretty soon they want me to do some traveling to some of our branch offices. I'll go—but oh, we've *got* to get a housekeeper. I guess, though, women's liberation hasn't affected me much. It has in the sense that I'm a lot less willing to be shoved against a wall by men, and it annoys me when I see my sister kowtow to the men, to the extent, for example, when Bob says, 'Let me help you with the dishes,' and she'll say 'Oh, no, no, I'll do them.' That kind of thing. But I'll tell you, I always want to stay free enough of things to give my job the finger anytime I want to."

Does Laurie's work bother Bob?

"No, not at all," he says. "She's happy doing it. The kids are loved and happy. It's okay."

It sounds a little pat, a little quick. Bob thinks for a moment and says, "Look, I'm not saying everything's perfect and all worked out. I still have my memories and she still has hers. We don't want any of it to happen again, and that makes us discuss things with each other a lot faster —any gripes or complaints at all."

"Yeah," says Laurie. "I bitch a lot more."

Bob stays earnest and doesn't smile. "Well, maybe you do," he says, "but I'm freer to talk about stuff, now. It's damn easy to fill my life with doing practical things, and not have an emotional life. But it's got to be there." He looks toward me and continues, "All my life I've had a hard time labeling and identifying my feelings. I didn't feel because I didn't give myself time to pay attention. Now I stop and ask myself—What is my real reaction to this? It makes it easier to communicate with Laurie."

He takes a deep breath. This has been almost a speech for him. "As I said, it doesn't always work out perfectly. But I'm able to say 'I'm sorry' or 'I'm unhappy' or 'I'm irritated.' "

What, I ask Bob, is the most irreplaceable part of this marriage?

"The most irreplaceable? I don't think there is any single

element that's irreplaceable." His brow furrows and he stares at the table. "Yes, there is. Time. The longer it lasts, the more irreplaceable it becomes."

Laurie speaks up quickly, lightly. "Probably the most irreplaceable thing in our relationship is your ability to put up with my shit. I don't know of anybody else who would. I mean, put up with it without being a patsy—"

Bob shoots an amused glance at Laurie, who looks quickly toward me. "I never walk over him, in case you haven't noticed."

How, I ask, would he describe his love for Laurie?

"Well—"

"Unthinking—how's that?" she jokes.

"It's mellowed," he says. "I love you in a passionate way, but it's less"—he looks for a word, shrugs helplessly—"it's less insistent."

And sex?

Laurie sighs. "Less than ideal."

Bob nods. "The biggest detriment is finding time," he says. "It's not a waning of ardor, particularly." He waits for a second, then continues, his mind back to the previous question. "I miss you when you're gone," he says to his wife. "I worry about you when you're flying somewhere or driving. You're so much a part of me and so important to me that I worry." He pauses. "Is jealousy a part of love?"

None of us has an answer. He continues, "I want to be with you, and I have an all-abiding concern for you and, sure, sexual desire. That's my love."

Touched, Laurie reaches out her hand and touches his face. "I worry about you too," she says. "I worry you'll be in a crash or something. When I think about my love for you, I think, 'He's so much nicer than that other person—aren't I lucky to have him?' " She pauses. "I'm sort of disappointed in our sex life now, but I don't do a whole lot to improve it. It seems as if it's best when we're at a crisis point, but we don't have many of those now. We have a good, easygoing kind of marriage. It's not that I'm worried about it, but occasionally it's just routine."

"I'm more tender than you are in an everyday sense," Bob says.

"Yes. And a much more sentimental person."

He grins. "Sort of a romantic, in a way."

"I feel that too," she says. "But I don't talk about it much, do I?"

"Well, you had plenty of chances to check elsewhere for what you wanted," he says. "Guess it's right here, regardless."

Hours later I walk with Laurie through a nearby park. She is ruminating, reflective. "I'm not sure what the effect of talking about all this will be on Bob," she says. "I know I got a knot in my stomach more than once." She is silent and we walk without words for a while.

"I hurt that man very much," she says. "When I'm honest, I wonder, Will I stay monogamous? I don't know. But I do know I want this marriage. I really want it. And so does he."

"Adultery," proclaimed H. L. Mencken in 1920, "is the application of democracy to love." He should be around today. It would probably tickle his acerbic funny bone to observe how quickly marriage in America, viewed this way, has become one of our most democratic institutions.

The philandering husband is no new item since Mencken's time, but the rapid increase of women who either have had extramarital affairs or intend to is unprecedented. And it puts an extra complicated set of pressures on marriage.

Laurie Kincaid committed (to use the traditional punitive verb) adultery much more often—and earlier—than any other wife I interviewed still living in a working marriage. Even in these more tolerant times, there are plenty of people who would hasten to slap a big red "A" on her forehead. Too much, too soon. Now, maybe Laurie is fated to be compulsively unfaithful; maybe she's an example of Strindberg's polygamous personality. But then again, looking at the surveys of adulterous women, I think she may be less atypical than she seems.

In 1972 a Playboy Foundation study showed 24 percent of wives under the age of twenty-four were having affairs (a 16 percent increase over Kinsey's earlier statistics for the same age group), indicating early disenchantment with monogamy among women. Linda Wolfe figures that close to 40 percent of married American women are unfaithful to their husbands (although she gulps hard on that one herself—"I hope it isn't that high," she said in a conversation). Still, after *Redbook* magazine's survey of 100,000 women readers under thirty-five, with one third reporting extramarital sex, it looks as if the traditional faithful wife could be a dying species.

Partly it's a sign of the times. Laurie's affairs came during the mid-sixties, a time when adultery among women was often more desperate than deliberate, more in response to that hunger for "more," and a feeling of being left out of the so-called sexual revolution, than anything else.

In the small insulated university environment within which I lived, adultery hit like a high wind in a leaf pile, leaving a lot of people by the side of the road with dazed looks on their faces after the excitement died down. The French are able to handle extramarital sex with some taste and style. Not us.

Very few of the marriages I knew survived where wife and husband trooped off to all-night encounter groups and tried forging "meaningful relationships" with other partners. In retrospect, how strange it seems. Friendships were broken irrevocably, tears shed, and marriages shattered; so many sensitive, intelligent people managed to be so stupid about their emotions. "We were like children," a woman I have known for many years, also a faculty wife, said afterward. "We wanted to be hip and free and married and secure, all at the same time."

By the late sixties, when much of the experimenting leveled out ("It wasn't any different with my neighbor's husband than with my own"), a clearer picture emerged of what adultery in marriage means. It's clearly a major issue, but numbers and statistics don't differentiate between one-night stands, long-term affairs, and compulsive bed-hopping. They don't convey the different physical and emotional reasons that propel women toward adultery. Nor do they bring much clarity to the subject when the American wife who stays faithful to one man begins to look abnormal. Lederer and Jackson warn against a jump-on-the-band-wagon impulse, pointing out that doctors, marriage counselors, and psychiatrists pronouncing on the frequency of extramarital sex are talking to people eager to share their experiences. They also point out there is no way to know how a pollster's bias influences an interviewee's response.

Now that all that is said, it's easier to talk about the reality of adultery and the reality of its impact on marriage. Is adultery even necessarily infidelity? Actor Richard Harris, newly married to a woman nineteen years his junior, announced to the press, "It's not important to me what she does as long as she's not emotionally unfaithful. Marriage isn't based on vaginal fidelity. A couple of hours in a bed, what's that?" A little whistling in the dark, perhaps, but he addressed an important issue: the impact of adultery on the partner. As author Joseph Epstein said (quoting French philosopher Alain), "The slap in the face takes the form of the man who receives it, not the one who gives it, so the true meaning of adultery is to be found in the heart of its victim."

Is the adultery of one's spouse, then, a mortal wound? Or is it painful but tolerable? On that depends much of its importance. The reactions of the so-called "injured party" to adultery are as varied as any other human emotions, and often just as unpredictable.

In C. G. Jung's view, a marriage without a high level of consciousness cannot produce a deep or important psychological relationship. But rarely can this happen without crisis. As Jung put it, there is no "coming into consciousness without pain."

And oh, is there pain with adultery! But it often occurs in marriages as a momentary crisis that focuses existing problems in a way nothing else could. It is the electric shock that sets all nerves on edge, but it doesn't necessarily destroy. The crisis it provokes may involve confrontation between husband and wife, or it may exist totally within the head of the unfaithful spouse. If, for example, a man embarks on an affair as a means of exploring unfinished questions about himself, questions that should have been dealt with in a different time of development, he may find the answers he needs without confessing his unfaithfulness.

But it's rarely that easy. As any man or woman ever involved in the deception of adultery knows, the secret affair is like a worm in the belly, eating away at self-respect. Most men and women marry assuming they will remain faithful, and when they commit adultery, they feel guilty. It doesn't have to violate some outward standard of morality. It is most painful when it violates one's own self-expectations, for the wedding-day promises are rarely false when made.

The guilt conditioning in our culture for sexual infidelity is particularly strong for women. In that vast, silent area of unwritten social rules, the man may stray but the wife must be above reproach, for the stability of the family depends on her constancy. When that social expectation is violated, disapproval ("How could she run around on her family like that?") descends as quickly as a heavy fog. That does not, of course, stop women from having affairs. But it surely has something to do with the fact that many of them report illicit sex is more inhibiting than exciting.

Laurie Kincaid walks through that fog with as much bravado as she can muster, and on the whole, she pulls it off. She doesn't escape the guilt conditioning, and she still, at times, expects the sky to fall.

Perhaps Laurie gets so few kicks out of extramarital sex

because of that fear of punishment which is rooted deep in religion, history, and literature. Women who commit adultery (consider Hester Prynne, Anna Karenina, and Madame Bovary) are women who lose all in the end, and somewhere that fear still exists in Laurie.

Laurie and Bob came through the actual adultery, but as she said so clearly, it's living with all the residual pain and resentments later that makes the difference. They don't have the emotional ability to wipe the ledger clean as much as other couples I have known. There is a wariness, an atmosphere that lies still and invisible in the corners of their house. There is hard and conscientious work going on between them.

Still, I couldn't help contrasting them with a couple in Virginia that went through a similar situation. The wife had a jaunty beauty that drew attention from everyone; she was the kind of woman who could pull a painter's beret down across one eye, grin, and look so delightfully wicked she drew every male's gaze on the street. Her husband, an employee at the Pentagon, was frequently absent on trips. He was the type of man you see rushing through every American airport every day: harassed, unpressed, gulping down a Scotch at the stand-up bar before catching his next plane. Work came first, and that didn't sit too well with the lady in the beret. She sought the comforting arms of a neighbor, then those of a co-worker of her husband. As time went on, she expanded the game of musical beds to the point where everyone knew what was happening. And finally, of course, her husband learned too, which was what she wanted all along. They had the classic confrontation scene over potato salad and hot dogs at the park, the children playing nearby out of earshot, and he demanded a divorce. So why has it been different for Laurie and Bob? Why can one couple survive deliberate and flagrant adultery and another cannot?

Laurie's unfaithfulness forced the two of them to take notice of each other in a new and painful way, which they were both willing to do. But the real sustaining balance is their natural trade-offs of needs. Bob is a very straight guy, the kind who has been known to fall asleep at dinner parties. Without Laurie, his world would shrink rapidly. She provides the spark, the social contacts, the energy to engage and experience, and he wants to be around that. And Laurie? She gets stability and security from Bob. "I'm better off married," she said repeatedly. Without marriage, she might fly into fragments. For her, it is the structure which allows preservation of her "good person" self-image. She says she doesn't miss taking advantage of opportunities for sexual adventure, but it's still very important to her to sparkle and shine in front of admiring men. It occurred to me that she has a strong fear of being left alone. Keeping a cadre of possible partners circling in a holding pattern reassures her. Bob shares that fear of aloneness. And so, living with Laurie, he has opted for the risk of possible emotional loss rather than full abandonment. In this sense, they are intriguingly well matched. It's also possible that accepting her as she is takes a burden off Bob sexually.

In another marriage, that of a West Coast sociologist and his schoolteacher wife, it was hard to tell whether the wife's adultery was cause or effect, but one thing was clear: he had little sexual interest. After a long day's work it wasn't unusual for him to find himself impotent in bed. The tension between them would begin to build at dinner (would things work this time?). He would get an erection, lose it, get it again, and then plead tiredness. She had one affair, then another. Her husband knew what was happening, and rather than force a crisis between them, it oddly seemed to resolve the one they already had. He is a shy man, reserved, who says he himself has done no "playing around." He is easily irritated by little things that go wrong—missing the right turn on the way to the beach, finding dirty dishes left in the sink, a hole in his sock when he's ready to go to work. He spends long afternoons walking by himself. He needs a great deal of privacy, and his wife has come to accept that. She is not at present involved in an affair, but that possibility hangs suspended. They remain very affectionate to each other; they hold hands walking down the street.

"This will sound strange," she says briskly. "If we had a more sexually passionate relationship, what would that cost us? We both want our freedom. I think my sex drive is greater than his, and I don't want that to become a threat. Everything has a price, and the price I pay is small, considering all the things we like to do together and to talk about."

Her matter-of-fact dismissal of the importance of a good sexual relationship makes me uneasy because it doesn't come to grips with anything. Yet they are married, intend to remain married, and profess themselves pleased with what they've got.

Laurie isn't the type to make the same type of concession, at least not consciously. Still, Bob's sex drive is either being carefully controlled or authentically low. Often after a long day at the hospital, he also is "too tired." Their best sex comes during long shared lunch hours at home, but Laurie doesn't push. She doesn't like to give reminders of her strong sexual appetites. Are they all that strong? I wonder. She told me her best and most satisfying orgasms have been with her husband. She has often found herself in bed, in the midst of sex with a lover, wondering about the patterns on the ceiling or whether she should plan a stew or chicken for next night's dinner.

My thought is that much of Laurie's unfaithfulness has been part of her own particular fantasy trip, a need to experience excitement with minimal risk. Most of her lovers have not been social or intellectual equals of herself or of Bob. In that way she eliminates the risk of their becoming too important—having made a mistake on that score only once. Her present pattern of many "harmless" flirtations is feeding the fantasy needs with the least risk of all. She thinks she needs this ego building more than she does a good sexual relationship with Bob, at least right now. It has plausibility, although I don't believe it, quite.

But Bob and Laurie have a number of connecting forces, not the least of which is the way they view their work. Bob is in a highly success-oriented profession, yet markedly devoid of ambition to make money. With Laurie's status needs, that would be a problem, except for the fact that she is able to earn a good salary. Her commitment to her work remains casual, so far. So it isn't a threat. And Bob is quite happy sharing the financial power base within the family. He demonstrates no great power needs of any sort within the marriage.

But clearly, there are unmet emotional needs. Laurie talks with tender amusement of Bob's "sentimentality," yet it makes her uneasy. "He gives me mushy birthday cards, and when we're out to dinner, he'll get emotional about how much he loves me, and tears will fill his eyes," she said.

This makes her uncomfortable in a way she doesn't completely understand. At the risk of extending the impact of her guilt over her adultery a little too far, I'd say it's because she doesn't feel she deserves it. But Laurie retains a balance on her reactions. She does love this gentle, square husband of hers. And he loves her. The two of them (definitely against the popular stereotype) have increased the strength of their relationship through their children. In the way that each expresses tenderness and warmth to the children, they reflect back to each other assurance that the capacity for continued caring is there. The children are in this sense conduits for affection between a man and a woman who are very different, but who convey a deep and shared need for each other which is fulfilled through their marriage. Whether this bond grows and deepens is a question for the future.

the world traveler...
and his wife

Liz and Peter

I first meet Peter Arthur on a long and tedious flight from Zurich to New York. What impresses me initially is a cheery exuberance, the type of attitude one is more likely to encounter in a first-time tourist than in a businessman who makes Atlantic crossings as routinely as many of us commute to the suburbs. He is not bored, overweight, drinking too much, or on the make—and although I know these are stereotype descriptions of traveling businessmen, there's enough truth in them that meeting an exception is refreshing.

We talk about many things, including his ordinary routine, which includes at least ten lengthy overseas buying trips a year. Peter sells leather specialty goods. He started a small business ten years ago which has grown steadily and essentially revolves around him, giving him both the satisfaction of complete control and the burden of never getting relief from exercising it.

He looks more like a college cheerleader than a man accustomed to the constant grind of business meetings: he is slightly built, with large eyes that look startled when he is thinking hard. He is clearly restive when physically confined. "I don't like planes," he says. He is a questioner, one who listens to the responses. He asks me about my work, about my book.

"Marriage? You're going to write about marriages that work?" A forkful of roast beef stays suspended in the air. He is clearly interested, and we talk. "You know," he says at one point, "my wife and I hardly know anyone any more who's been married longer than three years." This depresses him, as it does me. We eat in silence.

Only much later does our conversation go back to marriage as he tells me about his own. "We've been married thirteen years," he says. "Sometimes I wonder if we'll make thirteen more, but we're both in there for the next five or so, anyhow." Traveling, he says, is a strain for his wife, who remains home in Chicago caring for their two small children. It has brought some bumpy times. "We've had to work out what we share and how we share," he says, and then he adds, "Funny, something like this should be talked about by both of us." He turns to me with a thoughtful look. "Maybe Liz and I might have something to contribute. I'll talk to her about it."

Months later I call and ask if they are interested.

There is a pause. "Yes, we are," says Peter.

Peter and Liz Arthur live amid a small group of expensively renovated homes in the center of a high-crime neighborhood in New York City, surrounded by slums, the kind of upper middle-class urban enclave that horrifies suburbanites. They love their home. Their children are still young enough to roam on their tricycles only to the end of the block, and so they feel secure. They are liberal Democrats, involved in neighborhood projects, and proud of toughing it out in the city. They have an ample supply of money to make toughing it out worthwhile.

When I arrive Peter opens the door, looking uncomfortable. "Hello, there," he says. He doesn't look quite as much like a cheerleader as I remember him. He looks instead like a man who has just gotten himself into a business deal he isn't too sure he likes.

The home is filled with good contemporary paintings and expensive furniture, and it is, at this after-dinner moment, self-consciously tidy. I hear children playing, but I do not see them.

Liz Arthur is sitting on the sofa, looking very pretty and bright in a red silk shirt. She holds out her hand to me and introduces herself with a forceful, matter-of-fact manner that implies great confidence and togetherness and let's-get-on-with-this efficiency.

(Later Liz tells me, "I was scared to death," and Peter says, "Our friends thought we were crazy to talk about our marriage.")

Two little girls run in, gigglers, crisp in fresh nightgowns, ready to head for bed. Their parents kiss them, there are a few stern admonishments from Liz about turning the lights out right away, and they leave. It is so very ordered.

"We do order our lives carefully," Liz explains later. "We have to because Peter is gone so much. When he is home, I want things to run smoothly."

It's always been that way for Liz. Home was a dollhouse, and she was the doll, the only girl in a family that included three brothers. She was the late child in her mother and fathers' lives, the only one happy to sit demurely in starched pinafores and Mary Janes when friends came to visit, content with being admired. She grew up as the Little Lady, and she hoped for nothing else than a quiet, ordered life, a dream that quickly got hazy when she met Peter.

"He was so *energetic*," she says with a smile.

"And you were the perfect girl to marry," he responds.

That's the way it started out, each comfortably packaged for the other.

"Romanticism was a real killer for us," says Peter. "We had to survive that before we could have children."

Peter also had to survive the attitudes he brought to his marriage. Born and reared in a small Midwestern town, he was the only child of a much-traveled salesman father and a quiet, stay-at-home mother. Affection was not freely displayed or expected. Peter's memories are of a reasonably comfortable childhood in a home where his father made most of the decisions. On Saturdays, after traveling his route all week, Peter's father would sit at an immense old oak desk, his wife across from him, hands folded, and go systematically through a list of household and family matters she kept while he was gone. (Should we buy a new roof or patch the old one? Should Peter go to private school or the new public high school?) He would discuss each item, make a decision; check it off. His mother would nod. It was, of course, up to her to carry them out.

Liz and Peter met at college in a small town in northern Indiana, and Peter was shopping for a ring within six months. It was a tiny diamond, but it was the first one awarded (won? earned?) in Liz's sorority, and she displayed it proudly. She would sit at the long dinner table at night, talking calmly to a friend, aware of the envious glances from the other girls, feeling somehow better than them. Smarter. More mature.

"Married was definitely better," she says dryly.

They stuck it out until graduation, without sex—at least without actual intercourse. Many a time Liz remembers coming to orgasm, palms damp, hands trembling, sitting in front of the sorority house in Peter's '56 Ford. "Remarkable," she says. "Through layers of clothes."

Their parents and Liz's brothers all showed up for the wedding, almost the last time they ever congregated in one group.

"We're just not very close to our families," says Peter. "We don't want to be. I don't even know where my grandparents came from, and I really don't care." He shrugs. It is a quick and casual burying of the past. "The only things that matter are what happen with us right now. And tomorrow. What we were or what we did aren't so important any more."

Liz looks faintly skeptical, but she says nothing.

Peter answers her unspoken skepticism. "I'm talking about the ability to adapt," he says, "the ability to change your way of thinking about things."

She nods. "That's part of it. Still—"

He turns to me. "We used to put out a product in my business that had a life span of eight to ten years. That was twenty-five years ago. Then the life span became five to six years, then three. Now it's a year, because people are constantly demanding a change, and that gets frightening if you can't adapt."

Peter sounds now very much like a businessman. Does change threaten his business? Is he tight about it?

"Oh no, things are going very well," he says. He glances at his wife, waiting for her to complete the answer, to enlarge it.

"They're going well now for us, too," she offers.

But it took time.

It was just about eight years ago that Peter took his courage and cash in hand and bought a faltering leather-goods business, almost precisely the time when Liz gave birth to their second child. She was apprehensive. He was excited.

"I told her it would take a lot of traveling, a lot of long hours to get the company turned around, profit-wise," says Peter.

"I figured I could handle it, and I did at first," says Liz.

But Liz was used to being taken care of. She didn't like being alone. And "a lot" of work was an understatement. Peter worked an average of twelve hours a day, seven days a week for the first two years and Liz began having nightmares about Richard Speck.

"I was terrified of staying in the house alone," she says, "not just this house—anywhere. I had visions of murderers waiting on my doorstep the minute after Peter would get on a plane. I felt angry, very resentful, almost like I was being abandoned."

"God, at times I'd come home from Europe and Mindy would stare at me and say, 'Gee, I almost forgot I had a daddy.' How much guiltier can you feel?" Peter squeezes his hands together, pushes himself back in his chair.

Liz didn't talk much at first about her feelings to Peter,

because she didn't think he would do what she wanted him to do anyway—stay home. And even when he did . . .

"We were both exhausted," says Liz. "I was tired of talking to kids all day, and if I wanted to hear about anything, it was his business."

"That was the last thing I felt like talking about," says Peter.

"So we just didn't talk," continues Liz. "I don't think we were really aware of the pattern that was building."

Liz became increasingly resentful and certain that Peter was choosing his work over her. She would wander through the house, polishing, sweeping; she would sit idly on the sofa reading a magazine, staring out the window and brooding. What was her life going to be like? Who was she, anyhow?

Liz began to take her anger and confusion out on the children. Why did they drop jelly on the floor every bloody day? Why didn't they ever pick up their toys? When were they going to learn to hang up their coats?

One afternoon Liz walked into their playroom and started the by now habitual yelling. Mindy watched her without changing expression. When her mother finally calmed down, she looked at the floor and said, "I don't ever want to be a mommy. Mommies lead horrible lives."

"That was the clincher for me," says Liz. "I tried to talk to Peter. It wasn't that he wasn't willing to listen—"

"Oh, I was a good listener on other things," interrupts Peter. "But I played the role of parent with you most of the time—trying to help you, but not communicating much of myself back."

"Well, it never seemed like you needed it," answered Liz.

She turns to me. "Peter has a very positive view of life, and always seems convinced that everything will work out. I couldn't match that."

"I wanted to help," offers Peter. "I knew I had to figure ways of working less, but I couldn't do much less without losing everything we both valued that the business did for us."

Peter and Liz value a comfortable life, but more than that, as Liz knew at the time, Peter was the up, eager type of man he was because he loved his work.

And there it was. The classic Work as Rival situation that wives have such difficulty comprehending, if they themselves have no comparable passion.

"I absolutely *hate* housework," says Liz with finality, "and I'm not interested in having a career—just Peter and the children."

Peter at first tried the kind of enthusiastic efforts at empathy that worked well for him with friends and in business. "When I was in college I had a teacher who taught me more than I ever learned anywhere about dealing with people," says Peter earnestly. "He tried to teach us how to go out of ourselves, how to mentally put ourselves in other people's situations, so we could understand their reactions better. It was an American Civilization class and for the mid-term, he put a fire engine on his desk and said, 'If you were a Puritan living in Salem, Massachusetts, in 1680, and you saw this coming down the street, what would be your thoughts?' " Peter pauses. He shakes his head at the memory with clear admiration. "It was fantastic," he says. "We learned so much."

It didn't work with Liz. "I could understand what you were saying about your frustrations," says Peter.

"But not my emotions. You didn't comprehend that I did not really like me." For a moment, her voice makes my eyes water.

Peter sighs. "No."

"I found him so irritating," says Liz with a laugh. "He was so damn positive about everything."

Liz's housewifely compulsions had become, slowly, part of the "me" package she didn't like.

"Like giving a party," she says. "I would get very uptight. You know? I had this idea in my head of what the standards were, what I had to do to give an acceptable party. I figured if you didn't do it with china and crystal and candlelight and fifteen different pieces of silverware, it wasn't done right. I'd complain to Peter that I didn't want to polish all the silver, and he'd say, 'All right, *don't* polish the silver,' " Liz stops and looks at me, a flush on her face. "None of this probably seems very important unless you're a housewife," she says.

I shake my head. Any woman who has ever given a dinner party knows what she's talking about. She is reassured, and continues, "But the problem was, if I didn't polish the silver, I was a bad person because I wasn't entertaining the right way. It meant I didn't care enough about what I was doing." She laughs again, with remembered frustration. "I'd try and explain this to Peter, and then I'd want to punch him. He thought he was understanding, but he really wasn't."

Like many women, Liz began talking to a trusted friend, who, with her husband, lived near the Arthurs. For years the

four of them were very close. "We'd run over there to borrow something, they'd drop by to talk—that kind of thing,"
says Peter.

He stirs in his chair, moves restlessly, rubs his forehead.
"We all got too close," he says.

Why too close? Were they sexually involved?

"No," says Peter, "but after a while I felt they knew more
about what was going on in our marriage than I did, because Liz talked to her so much."

"They did," responds Liz calmly.

There were complicated feelings of jealousy, for Peter
began to feel shut out, not only from Liz but from the one
couple friendship that meant a lot to him. "I don't have
time for many friends of my own," he explains.

Over time, this couple had become closer to the Arthurs than any other people, including their families. "We
saw them almost every night when Peter was home," says
Liz. "When we moved to this house, they bought one
nearby and we got together at least twice a week. We were
very, very close."

"He was like a brother to me," Peter says suddenly.

The confusion of confidences began to run in another
direction when their friends began to have marital problems. Together, Liz and Peter tried to help, but within a
year their friends divorced.

"It jarred us a lot," says Peter.

In a particularly painful way the loss of that couple from
their lives sharpened their mutual feeling of jeopardy.

"That's when I decided to get help from a therapist,"
says Liz.

At first this frightened Peter. "Look, I come from a small-town background where anybody who goes to a shrink has got to be crazy," he says. "I felt we should handle our own problems."

But Liz walked out of her home one morning without scrubbing the floor or doing the dishes or picking up after the kids. She said goodbye to the baby sitter and drove downtown to keep the appointment that, ultimately, redirected their lives. She called Peter first and told him where she was going. That afternoon, Peter walked down the street to a bookstore and bought a stack of psychology books.

"I thought I had better try and get an understanding of what she was doing," he says.

That night Liz and Peter talked about her session with the therapist. "Twelve years before, I would have shut her off," says Peter. Instead, each session with the therapist ended with a talk at home. Peter went also, six or seven times, at the therapist's request. "I was curious, too," he says. "I never would have thought of going, but I could see how much good it was doing for Liz."

"The therapist got across to me that my whole fear of being abandoned and my anger at Peter for leaving me had to be dealt with," says Liz. "I had to quit pretending to accept it, because I was taking all my anger and transferring it to Peter and the children, convincing myself they were the hostile ones. Am I making sense?"

It is, in fact, the warmth and confidence in her eyes that makes sense.

Liz stayed in therapy for three years. Does she have any doubts about being the only one going or resentments that Peter didn't get himself off to a therapist, too?

"No," Liz says, with a very positive shake of her head. "It was my problem, not his."

"But we both benefited," says Peter. "That's the point."

Peter still works grueling long hours and he still travels about 25 percent of the time. Liz has made her adjustments. "I still don't like being alone," she says, "but I've learned to enjoy at least the first couple of days he's gone, doing needlework, visiting friends, things like that. And now I plan trips with the children to see our parents for the times when he's gone." She pauses. "Maybe all this sounds a little too determined, but it works for me. I know myself much better now. I'm not really interested in having a career, nothing that takes me out of my home for a long time. I just don't have any ambitions in that direction, so what I make of what I've got happens right here."

Peter made his adjustments too. "That's when we began carefully planning out our time together," he says. "When I'm home now, I don't pick up a newspaper or a book or anything until the kids are in bed. Then, after that, our time is our own. I used to play golf a lot on the weekends, and I gave it up. I haven't played golf now in seven years."

Ah, do I detect some noble self-sacrifice?

"Oh, maybe," Peter smiles, "but then—I've got tennis."

Liz rolls her eyes. "Which is something we love to play together," she says. "But it took some touchy moments."

It seemed at first like such a good compromise. The two of them, out on the courts together—and then they discovered the marital pitfalls of tennis.

"I guess it's like bridge," sighs Peter.

A real power game, right?

"Yep."

Each Saturday they would go together to the courts. Liz looked great in her tennis shorts, but her serve was awful. At first, Peter enjoyed playing teacher ("That's right, honey, bring up your racket! Turn your foot more to a forty-five-degree angle! Good girl!"), but as the Saturdays wore on and it became clear Liz would never be more than a mediocre player, his directives got sharper ("For God's sake, Liz, keep your eye on the ball, will you?").

"Peter's always been the teacher, and I've always been the child," Liz says suddenly. "That's what I've felt most comfortable with, in a way. But I hated those Saturdays. I hated the lectures and the tension."

They eventually ventured into the tricky business of playing doubles, with each other as partners. At this point, all politeness vanished.

"Peter is competitive and he can't stand to lose at anything," says Liz. She smooths back her dark hair, running lacquered nails through the ends. "Well, did we ever lose."

One August afternoon, under a sun so intense heat waves shimmered over the court, Liz couldn't get a decent serve across the net. Each time she tried and failed, her muscles grew tighter. Peter said nothing, the worst of all. He stalked from one side of the court to the other. And Liz, the Little Lady who never was allowed to muss herself up playing competitive sports, sweated and strained and tried to prove she could be reasonably athletic, reasonably competitive. And so they kept playing, the other couple politely silent, the tension between Liz and Peter as intense as the heat on the court.

They played and they lost, and at about the time Liz's

last serve hit the net, that one game had become an allegory for her marriage.

"My God, I hated myself," she says. "It was clear I couldn't do *anything*. I was embarrassed, and I hated Peter for making it so much worse with his disapproval."

Plunk. The ball was in the net. Peter threw his racket on the ground in disgust and whirled on Liz. "What's the matter with you?" he shouted.

Click. Liz wiped the sweat from her eyes and threw her own racket. The child was about to reject the teacher.

"I will never, *never* step on a tennis court with you again in my life," she said, and the fury underlining each word forced Peter back a step. The other couple tiptoed away. Liz stomped off the court. Peter stood there, nonplused. Teacher wasn't sure what had happened.

"We talked about it afterward," Peter says. He grins. "As soon as Liz got a shower and a gin and tonic, and cooled down."

She made no apologies. "I told him if he couldn't treat me with the same courtesy or respect as he treated a friend or even a total stranger out there, then it was no good for me," she says.

"It wasn't that I meant to treat you badly," says Peter. "I'd get wrapped up in the competition of it all—"

Liz says nothing.

There are any number of married couples who don't dare to play tennis together. It's like lifting up a rock, all sorts of things crawl out. Even talking about it doesn't do much good.

Peter thinks about that. He frowns, sort of a fake frown

in an effort to restrain his own natural optimism. "I'm sure that's true," he says. "But it worked for us. I respected Liz coming right out and saying what she felt. I—" He catches his wife rolling her eyes. "Well, I *was* pretty surprised," he finishes. Then brightens. "We're able to play together now."

"You loosened up, Peter, but my game got better, which helped." They laugh at the same time.

"I've got to admit, that took two years of lessons with a tennis pro," Liz adds.

So much for tennis. The Arthurs, at least, have survived this particular experience in togetherness. What about the balance of power off the court, in the home? How do they divide authority and responsibility?

"Well, at first, I believed a man was totally head of the house," says Peter. "I wasn't here very much, but I didn't want to give up control."

"Oh, God, like the plumber incident," sighs Liz.

"Yeah," grins Peter. "When we first got this house, we had a million things that had to be repaired. I'd tell Liz to go ahead and call the plumber and take care of it."

There is a short silence. Liz is thinking about Peter heading out the door in the morning, handing her a scribbled list, saying "Take care of it." She is thinking of all the hours spent waiting for repairmen who didn't come and she is particularly thinking of the day the plumber, due to arrive in the morning, who came at five and worked away at the kitchen sink pipes until six o'clock. She had waited at home, fuming, all day: no grocery shopping, no chance to get Peter's shirts to the laundry in time for his next overseas trip, and with tools spread around the kitchen floor, no chance to prepare dinner until after the plumber cleaned up and left.

Peter showed up that night at six-thirty. He was irritated because dinner wasn't ready. He snapped his newspaper open and mumbled when he found his shirts hadn't gone to the laundry. Then he looked under the sink, inspected the work, and decided he didn't like it. "Why didn't you tell him we wanted new piping for the whole thing?" he snapped.

It wasn't quite as spectacular as the tennis court scene, but Liz slammed a still-frozen chicken into the sink, turned to her husband, and said, "Okay, if you want the things in the house done exactly your way, then you come home and you take care of it."

"That kind of got to me," acknowledges Peter.

"You weren't interested in keeping track of the plumber or the electrician, but you didn't want to give up the power of overseeing me—overseeing *them*," Liz points out. It is a neat point.

Peter blinks and nods without smiling. "Well, that's still a problem," he says.

Liz presses. "Part of the problem used to be you never gave me enough money to pay for all the household expenses. I had to check with you all the time."

Peter perks up, responding, "That was dumb of me. I guess that's where some of the ideas of women's liberation finally got through."

One evening Peter and Liz sat down and drew up a realistic household budget, one that left Liz discretionary money. From then on, Peter gave her the full amount at the beginning of each month. "How I spent it and on what became my business," says Liz with satisfaction. "I stopped feeling I was on welfare. Or something."

Peter is thinking about money. He says, "At least we've got plenty. I make between fifty-five and seventy thousand dollars a year now, depending on investments."

"The only thing Peter checks me on sometimes is buying clothes. I go overboard once in a while," says Liz.

Peter does not disagree. "Basically, our attitudes about money are conservative," he says. "We feel the same way about buying what we buy, when we buy it. For instance, this house. Most of our friends were buying homes long before us, but we figured it was better to invest it back into the business and get a house later."

"Arguments about money? Not any more," adds Liz. "There's no pull or conflict there." She stops for a moment. "Sometimes I make a little money working with a friend in her craft store, and I like having some that is my very own. I keep a savings account, and Peter pays the taxes."

"I told her last month, 'Okay, no more buying for this season,'" says Peter. "So she kept buying anyway."

"But when the bills came in, I paid them," Liz points out.

"Right." Peter does not seem to mind. He seems pleased.

"I'm not usually out earning any money, though," says Liz. "Usually only during the times when Peter is gone."

We are back again to the primary "problem." Is Peter's traveling still defined as a problem?

Liz thinks for a short while. "Well, it's an accepted problem now," she says slowly. "It's part of our lives, at least for now."

Loneliness is not easy. And neither is fielding the reactions of friends and family when Peter is gone.

"It bothers me that many husbands call every night or every other night when they're out of town," admits Liz. "But Peter can't do that so easily when he's in Europe. I've tried not to let it become a big thing to me, and I try not to *ask* him to call."

"There's just no satisfaction in a telephone call," Peter protests. "It costs too damn much and it doesn't please me; it just frustrates me."

"You're basically not a telephone person," answers Liz.

"Well, remember last time—"

Liz nods. "I know, I know. Last time Peter called, he caught me in a lousy mood and we started to get into an argument on the phone. I didn't want to fight, but I couldn't seem to get control of the situation."

Part of what bothers Liz is the unspoken assumptions people make about traveling businessmen.

"They're all supposed to be running around," she says resentfully.

I remember fleetingly my own plugged-in stereotype short-circuiting when I met Peter.

"I used to be very envious of the things Peter was able to do and see when he traveled," Liz continues. "Who wouldn't want to be dining at a castle overlooking Salzburg instead of fixing hamburgers for kids in New York?" Her face clouds; she looks away.

"Well, honey, you're coming along with me more now."

"I know, and that matters a lot. But it's more than that—

it's trust. I know people having affairs, and they make comments about Peter—but I'm comfortable. I don't think about it."

Not at all? No twinges?

Liz looks matter-of-factly at Peter. "I don't think Peter would be unfaithful to me."

Peter's response is to lean forward and say, "I guess the thing I value most about our marriage is the combination of love and respect we have for one another." He hasn't directly answered the question wrapped in Liz's statement. She chooses to ignore that.

"We take each other for granted, Peter. I assume you'll be there when I need you."

"You're right, Liz. It's trust."

What about their children?

"We've talked about it, and we're really glad we didn't have them right away," says Liz. "Whatever mistakes we made, and whatever games we played in the early years, at least we had time to develop an allegiance to each other."

Peter smiles. "I like that word."

"It's like building the foundation of a house," says Liz. She laughs suddenly. "We can thank President Johnson for making husbands exempt from the draft instead of just fathers. If he hadn't, I probably would have gotten pregnant so Peter could stay out of the army."

"It would have been much harder," says Peter. "When we had our first child, our whole lives changed—you go from being free to enjoy each other to really being in jail."

"Particularly me," Liz reminds him dryly.

Peter nods. "You were the one stuck at home when I started building the business."

"Remember the apartment we were in when Mindy was born? I'd wait all day for you to come home, and we'd no sooner sit down at the dinner table than she would start to scream. It was like she knew this was my only time with Peter, and she'd say, 'Oh no, I'm not going to let you have it.' Sound silly?" Liz smiles. "I've got to admit I really resented the time she took away from us."

"It's much better now," says Peter, "but I can't figure why people have more than two children, and the fact that some of them have a child to solve their problems—" He shakes his head. "That amazes me."

"They get divorced," says Liz.

After a moment of silence Peter suddenly asks, "God, I wonder what our next crisis will be?"

Liz spreads her hands, palms upward. "Who knows? We'll have one or two or three, that's for sure."

"I don't think we'd want to get really close to a couple again," says Peter. "It's better for us. We have more friends now, but the relationships aren't deep."

"That's more satisfying to us," says Liz.

Peter tries to explain. "There's only so much of oneself a person has to give," he says. "We want to spend our time on our own relationship."

"You know what I think?" says Peter. "Schools should give classes in how to cope with problems when they come up. I mean, if anybody's really interested in solving this divorce problem, why don't they teach children what can be done? Prepare them for what is going to come?"

"We had no preparation," murmurs Liz.

"We just thought we did," her husband adds. "We had to learn how to argue."

"The incident on the tennis court was a little thing in a way," says Liz. "But it meant a lot for me to come right out and tell Peter I thought he was making fun of me when I was trying as hard as I could to play well."

"It wasn't so much the fact that she got mad," says Peter, "but there was this completely honest statement of how she felt." He shrugs. "Up until then, I never knew *why* she got so mad about playing tennis. I figured, okay, I didn't want her to feel that way, so I'd stop."

"We've done our share of game-playing with each other," Liz reminds him.

"Oh hell, we wrote the book," answers Peter. "Remember that awful fight we had in the kitchen a few years ago? We both threw ten years' worth of stuff at each other."

Liz looks up at Peter. "Like my not being a virgin when we were married."

Peter stirs a little uncomfortably.

"Well, I wasn't, either."

"But it bothered you. I was stupid and honest and, when you asked, I told you the truth."

"Yeah, I know. I was pretty provincial."

Liz and Peter didn't have a sexual relationship with each other until they were married, which was Peter's choice, not Liz's. "I wanted to be sure I was marrying the right girl," says Peter, a little self-consciously.

His wife laughs. "Honey, you had such rigid feelings about girls. Anyone who had her ears pierced was either a whore or a gypsy, and anyone who wore loafers without socks—"

"Okay, okay." He smiles sheepishly.

And their sexual relationship now?

"It's good," says Liz.

"Reasonably," says Peter.

But for the first few years after marriage, Liz was unable to have an orgasm. It confounded and frightened her, for hadn't she, after all, already proven her sexuality? Was she going to be frigid? Was it some kind of biological punishment for her premarital sex experience?

These were heavy questions, and like thousands of women before her, Liz chose to fake orgasm rather than tell Peter what was happening. ("That's a woman's ultimate power," a Chicago society leader married to an aging industrialist once told me with quiet satisfaction. "A man has only so many pops in him, but a woman can go on indefinitely.")

The problem eventually corrected itself, but it still upsets Peter that Liz never told him.

"I felt I had been making love for two years to a great actress instead of my wife," he says. He thinks about it. "Men don't have the luxury of that kind of deception."

When Peter began his heavy traveling schedule, their sexual relationship suffered, at first.

"We found one simple dumb thing made an enormous difference, giving us more time with each other," says Peter.

They look at each other shamefacedly.

Liz smiles. "A lock on our bedroom door," she says.

"I think sex may be better for us because we don't get into a dreary routine about it," says Peter, in his look-on-the-bright-side way.

"Oh, Peter, we still don't have enough time."

"You know what the real trick is to making a marriage

work?" Peter asks. "It's caring enough to try. The first time you don't try, it becomes easier to let things slide the second time a problem comes up. Then you try a little less, blame the other person a little more, and then you reach the point finally of not caring."

He stops and reflects. "When we began drifting apart, I got scared. What would happen to the kids if we split? What would life be like for them?"

Liz adds, "We don't know anybody who's been married for any length of time, besides ourselves. Every now and then our girls ask, 'Hey, Mommy and Daddy, when are *you* getting a divorce?'"

Liz smiles at her husband. "You know, Peter, I was just thinking about where I'd put our marriage on a scale of one to ten."

His expression turns expectant. "Well?"

"I'd rate it about eight and a half."

Peter laughs. "I would have said nine to nine and a half."

Liz shrugs. She makes no adjustments of the ratings.

"You know the one thing I'd change about you, don't you?" says Peter to his wife.

"Sure," she answers, reaching for her cigarettes on the coffee table, "my smoking."

"I ordered her to quit smoking when we were married," Peter explains, resignedly watching the smoke waft to the ceiling. "I even tried bribes. Then I just couldn't stand smelling the things, but now I'm worried about her health."

"Oh, that's stupid," retorts Liz.

"Smoking two to three packs a day is what's stupid," says Peter.

"Look, I have to honestly say I don't want to quit. I'm intelligent enough to realize if it were important enough to me, I would." Liz's voice is taking on the standard quit-bugging-me tone of the confirmed smoker under attack.

"It's irrational," mutters Peter.

"I know it," she says calmly, and then, turning to me, "I went to a hypnotist for a while—didn't work."

And what irritates Liz about Peter?

She pauses, flushes. "He picks his feet when he gets nervous at night."

"Hey!" protests Peter.

"Well, you do," she says. "It bugs me. And you ignore your health, too."

"Look who's talking!"

"Well, at least I don't pick my feet."

They glare at each other for an instant. Then Peter laughs and slaps his hands together. Liz leans back, inhales deeply, looking both triumphant and embarrassed.

Now that they have made clear what is imminently replaceable, I ask what is irreplaceable in their marriage.

"That's harder," says Peter. "I guess I have to try and say what love means to me." He is silent for a moment. "It means mainly caring about what Liz feels and showing I care, I guess. The irreplaceable part? We really like being with each other and with our kids. I'd hate to be without that. We've built up feelings of warmth and liking . . ." He stops, shrugs. "Anything's possible these days. I suppose we could get to a point where we'd want a divorce, but I can't conceive of it."

"I feel the same way," says Liz. "We'll just have to keep talking and sharing our feelings and things we like to do, and preparing for the time when our kids are grown and gone."

"Maybe that'll be the next crisis," says Peter.

"Well, let's hope we'll still have plenty to say to each other then."

The evening has gone. We are deep into morning, and Liz suggests a move to the kitchen for coffee and cake.

"Did you feel a little unwelcome when you came?" she asks as we walk to the kitchen.

I acknowledge that I did sense a slight chill.

"This morning I woke up from a horrible dream," she confesses. "I dreamt you were here and asking questions and we were talking and then Peter said something terrible about us that I hadn't realized he felt and everything came crashing down."

Her smile is slightly teary-eyed and Peter puts his hand on her waist, giving a quick squeeze. "Didn't happen, did it?"

"We've got a good balance going, Peter. And a lot of that is because of you. I love you for it."

I felt comforted by my interview with Liz and Peter Arthur. It's an odd word, I suppose, but they had a constancy about them that left me with the feeling that when I walked out of their front door, I wouldn't look back and find they had suddenly vanished, their marriage gone without a trace. I've had nightmares of this happening with some of the couples I've interviewed.

I suppose this sense of comfort was partly because Peter impressed me with his willingness to stay ahead of Liz's need for change. (The image of him running out to buy psychology books when she started therapy was, in a way, endearing.) What he has done is take on the role of being the change agent in this marriage, no small task for the person who had it made already. Married life was very comfortable for Peter: he had the opportunity for traveling to exciting, exotic places on the one hand, and the security of coming back to a stable, secure home on the other. It was definitely a case of being able to have one's cake and eat it, too, and many men, unlike Peter, indulge in preposterous mental gymnastics, trying to deny their wives' unhappiness when life, as far as they are concerned, is quite all right, thank you.

I'm reminded particularly of people I knew long ago in Los Angeles. His job was exciting and absorbing, as Peter's is, while hers had turned into a never-ending trap of raising the children, cleaning the house, and cooking dinners that dried up in the oven on the frequent nights when he didn't make it home in time. She began taking Saturday afternoons off and going into town to sit in a dark movie theater by herself, wanting him to ask what was wrong. He ignored her. When he was home, she took to going out in the evening, announcing she intended to be "out" for three hours. No explanation. He pretended it was all quite normal, and that she was, of course, visiting her sister, even though she came back with swollen eyes after sitting in tears through a double feature. She took to screaming at the children; then screaming at him.

Even when, finally, the two of them ended up visiting a marriage counselor, the most he could acknowledge was, well, maybe she ought to take an evening class at the local college or something. But anything seriously wrong? Anything that involved change from his side of this marriage? No, no. It was her problem. Not that he wasn't willing to "help," from a distance. And that of course is the way things ended up. The two of them, very much distanced, very much divorced.

I give Peter Arthur top marks for positive selfishness. He loves his exciting life even while feeling guilty about it, but he wants more from marriage than a stable environment to anchor him. Repeatedly he talked about his anxieties over rapid change: products obsolete as fast as they come on the market; friends' marriages with a shelf life about that of overripe cheese. Instead of being swept up into rootlessness by his hundreds of hours of jet travel every year, he questions the effects of rapid pace. Whatever the triggering mechanism was inside of Peter, he has forced himself to change in order to conserve the more fundamental parts of his identity, in order to avoid the greater loss.

The rootlessness of the traveling businessman is a common problem in marriage. I have watched and talked with a number of men who live forever on airplanes, who are more used to hanging their hats in a Holiday Inn than in their own homes. They can't handle the disapproval of their wives, nor do they quite understand what all that traveling does to them. One afternoon at Washington's National Airport I met a couple from Sarasota, Florida, the two of them cheerfully off on their first vacation together with their two children in a year. Through them, I got another glimpse of how people with a working marriage handle the problem of long absences. Jim, the husband, was gone four days out of every seven, traveling to three or four cities, and he hung his hat in many a Holiday Inn. How did he keep personal stability? "I establish mini-homes in the different towns," he said. "I try to stay in the same room at the same hotel, go to the same restaurant for dinner. I even have a jogging route established around one hotel I stay at in Columbus, Ohio."

His wife, a tall brunette with golden skin tanned through long daily hours on the tennis court, said she hated Jim's traveling routine and fought it hard the first year. "Now we've established a pattern of being together and being apart that suits us beautifully," she explained. "When he used to get home late for dinner, I would get angry and things would be tense. Now I'm never left waiting. When he's gone, he's gone. And when he's home, he's really home."

Liz Arthur never met the couple from Sarasota, but that's the kind of consistency she has accepted for herself. Not without a struggle. If Peter announced tomorrow he was going to quit all the traveling, she would be a happy woman, but she doesn't expect that. She has made her basic accommodation to keep the marriage going.

I don't quite buy her insistence that it was all her problem, though. The way she looks at Peter is sometimes too carefully controlled. Liz Arthur still wants to be taken care of in a more traditional way than Peter's life style allows. And she's jealous of all the glamour. Who wouldn't be, sitting home on a cold night with two demanding children, dreaming of one's husband in an elegant restaurant in Florence? When I asked her whether she was worried about Peter being unfaithful, she watched him very closely as she spoke of her trust; in such a way, it came out as Trust with crossed fingers.

The contrast between Liz's self-containment and Peter's enthusiastic, positive problem-solving attitude struck me at some points as being a very good balance, and at other times as being a factor in her guilt feelings about not "adjusting" better. Liz still expects herself to somehow come out perfect. Her home is carefully clean, carefully decorated. The paintings are color-coordinated with the furnishings, and even the children, in bright nightgowns and with shining blond hair, look as if they were hand-picked for the setting. It's the type of compulsiveness that any housewife might easily understand, but it's also a consuming thing. Here again, Peter is a jump ahead. Last winter he took Liz on a vacation trip to the Orient, and then gently prodded her into taking on some business responsibilities. She tentatively began searching out new sources, and then did some buying on her own. Liz says she enjoyed participating in Peter's work. That pleased him. He plans to take her again in the fall, give her more responsibility, and gradually weave her into the pattern of his work life as the children grow older. That's a good-sized step for a man who started out with the very traditional views of husband-wife roles that Peter did.

Although Liz proclaims her commitment to the home, she is both compulsive and restless. And defensive, too. The full-time housewife today is all too aware of society's low esteem. No economic value is placed on her work. The arguments for the injustice of this attitude have been repeated thousands of times, but a few of the facts behind them are worth repeating once again: the value of the services of housewives has been calculated at roughly one-fourth of the total Gross National Product. The average housewife, to break it down a bit, does about $257 worth of work a week, or some $13,364 a year. The fact that she has become part of a massive servant class, says economist John Kenneth Galbraith, is "an economic accomplishment of the first importance." For if she ever got paid for all her work, the economy as we know it would collapse. *Paying* for somebody to clean the floors, drive the kids to school, fix the vacuum cleaners and cook the food? Housewives, suddenly, would become the largest single category in the labor force. It is not likely, but what our society doesn't value economically becomes diminished socially and psychologically.

So Liz Arthur's restlessness is understandable. She doesn't want payment for what she does at home. But she doesn't want her own compulsiveness to eat her from the inside out either. She is taking small, important steps away from the relentless socialization of her childhood to a traditional marriage, breaking down the habit patterns of the Little Lady who became the Big Lady. But women in this situation must prepare themselves to be autonomous, to quit hiding behind their husbands' bankbooks and names if marriage is to work. It can be done, Liz and Peter are convinced, without throwing away the values of maintaining a home, even the pleasure of having a clean kitchen floor.

But their expectations can go too far, all the way to the Superwoman syndrome: the "expert" who makes every woman trying to juggle work and home feel like a failure. Women who overlay one set of responsibilities with another without relaxing their compulsively high standards are responding to the fact that they feel judged on two fronts. The prime motivation for Superwomen seems to be guilt.

Liz Arthur isn't at that point. Yet.

As far as sex is concerned, Peter is still not totally freed of his traditional views. It bothers him when Liz frankly discusses masturbation and, although he's embarrassed about it, the fact that Liz had sexual experience before marriage still doesn't seem quite right. It struck me in talking with Peter how many manifestations there are, among otherwise sensible, liberated men, of the age-old fear of woman's sexuality. Nineteenth-century doctors warned men to be careful of too much intercourse; somehow the loss of sperm was supposed to diminish a man's potency. Perhaps because the sexual attractiveness of women was seen then as a threat, Americans began to romanticize the male loner —the cowboy, the brave hunter.

Women were not supposed to enjoy sex. They were supposed to spend most of their lives girdled, trussed, and heavily skirted, undressing only in the dark, and if they were "ladies," they acquiesced to their husbands' advances, but they did not initiate their own. This view was so deeply ingrained that Dr. J. Marion Sims, the nineteenth-century father of gynecology, saw nothing wrong with the idea of using general anesthesia on women suffering from vaginismus (vaginal contractions preventing penetration by the male penis) so that their husbands could enjoy their own sexual experiences. Surgical removal of the clitoris was considered good preventive medicine—otherwise who knew what might happen if the female's sexual desire ran rampant?

The fear of an aroused woman who would force a man to

waste all that precious sperm, writers Helen Singer Kaplan and David C. Anderson point out, is probably based on "a simple and devastating fact of life: a man's capacity for orgasm is limited, while a woman's is not."

We aren't all that removed from these fears, in this sexually matter-of-fact society of ours. They play a role in the uneasiness of a man like Peter Arthur, which makes his willingness to risk change even more interesting. For whenever it is the husband making the major accommodations in order to maintain a working marriage, almost without exception he is risking his socially and culturally more powerful role. Who, in such a position, wouldn't be uneasy?

In more than a few ways, there are comparisons to be drawn between the Arthurs and the Steins: two men, Peter and David, both engrossed and guiltily delighted in their work; two women clinging to comfortable home roles for security, but still wanting more. (Liz's "more" is less focused than Jan's, but this will come, I think, in a matter of time.)

If I had to live in one of those two marriages, I asked myself, which would it be? After some thought I decided that if the luck of the draw gave me Peter Arthur as a husband, I'd feel better about future change. On the other hand, there's something solid about the way Jan and David square off at each other, something sturdy. Jan's highstrung nature and fighting temperament keeps David aware of her almost always, and that's a style Liz couldn't handle. But Peter keeps more of an eye on his own emotions than David. He's more aware of what he loses if everything in the marriage goes awry. And without the added problem of being a public personality, he is better able to stay in touch with his real self. ("I get out of the shower in the morning, look in the mirror, and I know I'm not special," Peter said. "I've got a rim of fat hanging over my middle and bowed legs. That's me. That's okay.")

What makes the accommodation work for this couple, as opposed to those marriages where long absences destroy continuity, is their determination to keep working out each problem, each resentment, as it comes along. Therapy helped Liz enormously. She's developing the self-confidence to initiate arguments on the basis of what's bothering *her,* instead of on the basis of what's wrong with *him.* That gives Peter enough positive feedback to keep marching up to the unknowns of change, rather than avoiding them.

Yes, they comforted me. I'm almost willing to bet money on their making it.

conclusion

It is May 17, 1975, and I am sitting in a Chicago movie theater, viewing Ingmar Bergman's *Scenes from a Marriage,* wondering whether I wouldn't rather be at the dentist getting my teeth drilled. It might hurt less, for I feel as if I'm walking back over the coals of my own marriage—and not only my own. The story of these two characters, Marianne and Johan, touches on the stories of many other marriages I have seen—the angers, pain, pleasures—even the specifics of this relentless, honestly drawn relationship on the screen are true to life.

But it is the final scene that I know I won't forget. Marianne and Johan have divorced and married other people, but as the years go by, they keep coming back into each other's lives, trying to understand their own relationship. Finally, as they lie together one night in an abandoned summer cottage, one says wonderingly to the other, "We are the best of friends."

And they suddenly realize much more. Says Johan, "It just struck me that you and I have begun telling each other the truth." Marianne turns to him, astonished, and says, "Didn't we before? No, we didn't. Why didn't we? That's odd. Why are we telling the truth now?" She thinks about it and then she says, "I know. It's because we make no demands."

JOHAN: We have no secrets from each other.
MARIANNE: Nothing to guard.
JOHAN: In other words, we can tell the truth. After twenty years.
MARIANNE: After twenty years.

I saw that movie at about the time I found myself fascinated by the mysteries and complexities of private lives. On certain days I walked out of people's homes feeling drained and wistful for the old romantic fictions, and yet realizing how infinitely more interesting the realities are.

I knew, of course, that there would be no ultimate reasons why some marriages worked and others failed, but there seemed to me to be basic underlying themes:

In the first place, these men and women see marriage primarily as a process, part of the changing landscape of their lives. They claim they would not be destroyed if it ended, because they see themselves not only as part of it but as separate from it. "Probably most everything could be replaced," said David Stein. The others echoed this, in other words.

They are not highly romantic people. Interestingly, the men tend to be more romantic than the women. It's a Laurie Kincaid or a Jan Stein who gets embarrassed by what she calls "mushiness," and tends to draw back. Although the fantasizing of the fifties definitely played a part in when and whom they married, it didn't run deep enough to destroy or distort reality. There is a strong chord of healthy selfishness in what they say and do. They also have the ability to tackle crisis rather than to avoid it. They accommodate each other, but not to the point of pretending.

Role confusion is not as much of a problem as it is in many contemporary marriages. In general, there is a traditional division of labor and responsibility, even when the wife works outside the home. But role ambivalence is another matter, because each couple is struggling with change, trying to stay a little ahead of the need for it. They are willing to experiment, but sometimes it scares them, and they become uncertain.

Yet with the exception of Jim Lowell, a man overwhelmed by outside change, these people are basically flexible. They bend to what needs to be done, from Peter Arthur to Bob Kincaid, from Jan Stein to Dorine Brosky. They have adjusted to radically different work schedules, freer sexual attitudes, or the women's movement, and when they've sensed too large a tidal wave coming in their direction, they've had the necessary internal mechanisms to retreat. Phil and Diana Morris have retreated the most, both in where they live and how they live, but they all manage to distance themselves both from outside family members and from friends. That surprised me initially, for one of the standard criticisms of the nuclear family is its isolation from a broad base of support systems. These people don't want such support.

I thought some of the women perhaps would have intense reactions to the women's movement, but most of the time they shrugged off questions that involved responding within some kind of general or ideological perspective. They were certainly concerned about their own situations, their own sense of importance within the home or through work, but they always saw these as specific to themselves. But none underwent convulsive identity changes after marriage—and that's important. The one aspect of women's liberation that really sparked a response was friendship. "It's much easier to really talk," said Jan Stein. "I've never felt able to be so honest with other women as I am now." Some of the others described it differently, but what impressed me the most about their enthusiasm was the sense of breaking out of a life-long isolation from other women.

I didn't find many couples initially comfortable talking about the balance of power within their marriages. The word "power" is loaded with negatives, and many of them instantly started equating it with conflict. So I asked them instead how they bargained with each other for position, for space, for attention, for whatever was important to them. One woman described it laughingly as sitting on a seesaw ("Sometimes it's my turn, sometimes his"), which was a pretty good description. The point that came through clearly to me was that they faced each other constantly on that seesaw, combining two of the other characteristics mentioned earlier: a strong sense of their own individual selfish interest and the willingness to tackle a problem they didn't want to let pass.

Money, which can play a pretty big part in marital power struggles, was rarely an issue. Dorine and Bert Brosky don't feel they have enough of it, but they don't quarrel over either their short- or long-term spending plans. Only with Jim and Anna Lowell did money play a serious part in the negative chemistry of the marriage, for Jim's diminished sense of self-worth couldn't handle Anna's paycheck carrying the family. That wouldn't be easy for most men in this society, but for Jim it was devastating. After listening to and observing these couples, I'm inclined to think that money problems, where the use or misuse of it becomes a weapon, is more a factor in marriages that are in real trouble than in those that are working.

Where money was less of a problem than I thought it would be, parenthood was more. I don't think it's at all incidental that (with the exception of the Broskys) every one of these couples postponed having children until after at least two years of marriage. They had the chance to get to know each other. They were not parents before they were comfortable in marriage. Even then, at some point in many of the interviews, I heard one or the other say that, maybe, just maybe, it hadn't been a good idea to have children. Dorine and Bert have the hardest time with this because they really had no choice. But all the others struggle with it too, and they are apprehensive about how their children will turn out. ("Even if we do everything right, we have no guarantees," said Phil Morris.)

The positive side of this is that very few couples I interviewed with working marriages had their egos wrapped around their children. They don't worry about how the kids will reflect back on them as much as I have seen with older parents. Partly they've seen what happened in the mid to late sixties when, for a while, it seemed as if a whole generation was dropping out or freaking out, and the standard American tactic of blaming it all on the parents didn't hold up. Another thing I noticed was that couples with working marriages complained more freely about their children than those with shaky marriages. (Could it be that children are a more integral part of troubled families than working ones? They are, in the sense that using them as a focal point takes attention off the center. In my own experience, and that of many other divorced parents, you can go for years talking with each other about little else than the children, using them as a physical and emotional buffer zone. If that's what you're doing, you don't complain about them without risking the loss of that buffer zone.)

A good sexual relationship is usually high up on the list of prerequisites for a working marriage. It is important, but as Carl Rogers points out in *Becoming Partners: Marriage and Its Alternatives,* it isn't basic. These couples described it as part of the ebb and flow of their relationships, but never as *the* or even *a* critical link holding them together.

Although good sex may keep some otherwise mediocre marriages together temporarily, it is a shaky bond, for good sex alone is replaceable. On the other hand, mediocre sex can erode a relationship seriously. But it doesn't end a marriage unless there are deeper problems. Part of the resentments expressed by these couples about children was that their needs interfered with sex at too many of the wrong times. "On Sunday morning, I want to roll over and make love and then sleep until ten," said Liz Arthur. "But the kids are always there, clamoring for breakfast." They want sex and they want better sex, but they don't rate it high on their lists of priorities. They aren't caught up in the compulsion to set performance standards that Dr. William Masters and Virginia Johnson have warned about—one more way these couples seem to side-step current trends.

And adultery? Even when they've had to deal with it, they don't accept it. "It's not so much the sexual unfaithfulness," said David Stein. "It's the lies you have to tell and the fact that there's a secret you can't share." None of them have let adultery become a cataclysmic event in their marriages. They've hung in there, long past the point where many couples might give up.

Basically, they want monogamous relationships and none of them are currently involved in affairs, or so they say. I hardly think, given the fact they clearly consider their marriages more important than this book, they would confess to existing, conflicting loves. But they have built histories of confronting each other in times of crisis, and this works to their advantage. As Laurie Kincaid put it, "We've put too much of ourselves out on the line dealing with all the screwing around I did before. We talk. We're honest. We'd want to keep it that way."

These couples have lived together through the most tumultuous years of the human sexual cycle, moving out to the farthest point of sexual polarity, with different needs at different times. With a little luck, now, as they enter middle age, they have a chance to keep it together. They have a better focus on the real issues that lead to adultery, and they are at least able to understand that a conflict between wanting monogamy and sexual adventure isn't unique to them. "Everyone is guilty of thinking there must be more," writes

Merle Shain. "More excitement, more ego gratification, more status and more fulfillment—and everyone is innocent of the knowledge of what the more will cost."

Sacrificing the commitment, the richness of intimacy hard won, is for them a steep price to pay at this point in their lives. "Those couples who enjoy trust, who give trust to each other," says Lederer and Jackson, "probably are among the most fortunate people alive." Whether it works out that ideally for them or not, they value it.

What about their work? The men in general are doing what they want to do, although the satisfaction level varies considerably. The women are, too. But there are interesting differences.

All of these couples are between thirty-five and forty-five, the time when men and women alike become acutely aware that life isn't going to go on forever. "Sometimes I wake up at night and think about being past the halfway point of my life," said David Stein, "and I get horribly depressed." These are the years when many men I have met find themselves looking down the other side of the mountain they spent so many years climbing. Often their wives, on the other hand, are seeing options they never dreamed were possible. The children are all in school. They have more freedom. They get excited by possibilities, while their husbands get depressed at the prospect of nothing but a long gray line of Monday mornings at the office.

That all of the wives profiled have worked at some point outside of the home—and plan to continue to do so—reflects one of the most important changes in marital life styles. Only Laurie Kincaid and Anna Lowell have what might be called careers, in the sense of full-time work focused on a development pattern that goes beyond job satisfaction or collecting a weekly paycheck. But the other four take pleasure and a sense of identity from work too: Diana's teaching is only partially satisfying, but her enthusiasm for midwifery is strong. Dorine dismisses her clerking as "only a little job" but she enjoys meeting new people. She likes an expanded world. Liz Arthur is discovering her talents as a businesswoman don't have to interfere with her view of herself as primarily a woman at home. And Jan Stein finds teaching an important source of self-confidence.

Work outside the home now and in the future will play a far more important role in their lives than it has in the lives of married women of previous generations, a fact their husbands have mixed and sometimes uneasy feelings about. "Jan's work has made our lives better because she's happier," said David Stein. "Not easier, but better."

The domestic stress for a marriage where both partners are working outside the home puts heavy pressure on traditional roles (Who's home to cook the chicken soup when Daddy has the flu? Who picks the baby up at nursery school when Mama has a board meeting?). But the economic dependency of women in marriage has had devastating effects on both the individual and the institution. I've seen so much anger and resentment, so many marital breakdowns caused by women becoming aware of this, that to entertain the fancy that a "good wife" can continue to program economic helplessness into her life is just to point the way to future marital disaster. Working women are undeniably better off. They have fewer mental breakdowns, fewer depressions, nightmares, headaches, dizziness. For better marriages, women need to be socialized differently. They need to rid themselves of the idea that marriage and motherhood knits up all the troublesome edges of their lives, that it is an ultimate protection. It is not.

Although the women I interviewed rarely stressed this, it was clear the women's movement has affected their views of work. They aren't particularly ideological or even focused in their views on liberation, but they have been profoundly affected by the idea that life is larger than the confines of one's home.

So why did they rarely see this influence of the women's movement as important? Partly because it hasn't brought divisive change. Most of these couples have not felt change forced on them. Ironically, because the women's movement isn't seen as a threat, it isn't seen as important.

And what about the men? As said earlier, the men seem much less satisfied with their work than their wives. Phil Morris' deep fear of failure and hunger for success doesn't amount to high job satisfaction. Bert Brosky likes the status of being foreman on the job, but his basic satisfaction is still the paycheck. The only two men who showed enthusiasm for their work were David Stein and Peter Arthur, but they also feel guilty about the consuming pace.

I frequently noticed that the wives would inject what I began to think of as "life-reminders" into the conversation when their husbands spoke of work dissatisfaction. They would bring up family picnics or status rewards or even a movie recently seen in order to remind the men that, yes, life was larger than just time spent on the job. The husbands seemed to need it. In one way or another, they all were dealing with some version of midlife disillusionment. (And their wives conveyed at times at least a trace of guilt over their own work enjoyments, an interesting twist on the old story of Man Busy Doing Meaningful Work While Wife Gets Left by the Wayside.)

Finally, a pattern I saw repeated time after time was active interest in each other. These people are not boring and they are not bored within their marriages. It's worth repeating, because it's so important: when Laurie Kincaid talks to her husband, he is interested. When Peter Arthur talks to Liz, she is listening. It's too hard to fake that kind of involvement for very long. (Remember the old game of looking around the restaurant, and figuring out who's married and who isn't? It's the people staring into space, eating across from each other in silence—these are the ones we tag as tied together for life.) Additionally, these couples tend more often than not to share some interest neither within the home nor related to work. Sometimes it was sailing, tennis, a book discussion group, or a commitment to working toward better schools for their kids—it didn't matter. Whatever it is, it enlarges their shared realm of experience and adds to their interest in each other.

I came away from these couples with new ideas about what dooms some relationships from the beginning and what allows others to work. In the first place, I'm totally awed by the self-defeating process of courtship. Two people come together at a point in their lives where there seems to be an alignment of expectations and needs that promise fulfillment, sexually and emotionally. Hearts beat fast;

there's some singing in the rain; some planning for the un-marred rosy future; and total entrapment in what Lederer and Jackson call the "ecstatic paralysis" Nature so cleverly designed to keep us all reproducing ourselves. Sometimes a couple will marry for security (which always assumes "for better" and not "for worse"); sometimes to alleviate loneli-ness (finding then that it's worse to be lonely with someone that it is to be lonely alone); and sometimes because of so-cial expectations ("What else do you do with yourself when you're already turning thirty?" asked one nervous man on that turning-point birthday).

Another motive that causes every bit as much trouble is expecting marriage to perform as a projection medium of what a person might want to be. People will marry to im-prove themselves by marrying someone with qualities they admire and wish they had, looking to complete themselves, to leap over their particular deficiencies. "I want," a single woman once told me with hunger and wistfulness, "to find a man who is large and wise and better than me."

It's only fair to add that I've never met anyone who man-aged to keep his or her head on straight through courtship. In the working marriages I've seen, the one thing that seems to derive from all the nonsense is recognizing the need for each human being to retain a private self. These couples have learned to step back from intruding on this sense, even when "letting it be" stirs fears of rejection and loss. It means a man resists the tendency to take control, and a woman resists the tendency to be subtly controlling. It struck me recently in a joking conversation after a wedding that the biggest power exercise for many women in life is persuading a man to marry them. Some never learn; witness this sour but apt description by Midge Decter of Courtship Two in *The Liberated Woman and Other Americans:*

> . . . Hardheaded as our divorcee has become, nevertheless for a while she will deceive herself and her new lover about the nature of their affair. She will feel too keenly the costliness of permanent commitment to admit that she is leading him into marriage. They will have fun together, she will say, and be friends, and she will demand very little of him and allow very little to be demanded in return.
>
> . . . Of course, she will make inordinate demands on him, and he on her; of course they will not be—never were—friends in the way she means. Soon the fun will go out of just being together, and she will tend to get querulous about the need to be discreet . . . She will grow afraid of losing him. One day she will place the ultimatum before him, and he will capitulate. Still, her early deception will bespeak a sort of ideal vision of their future together.

Lovers still hurry themselves along, systematically and covertly consuming, without learning the rhythms of togetherness and privacy they will need for a reciprocal marriage. The whole point of courtship gets lost in the haste to get past its uncertainty, and this business of allowing private places is very difficult to understand.

I've come away from this study with a new respect for people who can accept and then put aside painful memories. "Only by acceptance of the past will you alter its meaning," said T. S. Eliot, and that certainly holds true for marriage. Any union that lasts over a few years can't possibly be free of resentments and problems, but "keeping book" just builds the pressures. I've also come away with a better understanding of how mutual acceptance operates. It is right at the core of working marriages, and those who claim it comes only when two people don't give a damn about each other any more miss the point. That isn't acceptance, it's lack of interest. These couples have an acceptance of each other going, certainly with an ebb and flow, but it's based on a reasonably clear understanding of what makes the other operate. How to put this?

Perhaps the best way is with an example of how one pair, married now twenty-five years, handled a crisis that came their way at a point when he was absorbed in work and she was trapped with three small children at home. A chemist, he was working on a series of experiments that absorbed him completely. "For a time there, I seriously neglected her," he says.

And this is how he tells the story: "Sharon got so fed up that she called in the Quakers to advise her on whether or not to get a divorce. They were clearly scandalized by her story. I'm sure she painted it quite fairly; she really doesn't overdo things. They advised her strongly to divorce me, and said they would help, which is very odd for the Quakers. Curiously enough, instead of heartening Sharon, she decided she would not divorce me unless she could make me really feel the loss. She embarked on one year of spoiling me absolutely rotten. Oh, she intended to go through with it, but first she wanted to teach me what appreciation means." He smiled, and continued, "I'd bring unexpected guests home for supper, and rather than raise a complaint, she would produce a gourmet meal. I'd have to go somewhere, and she'd pack my suitcases with such niceness, such sweetness, that it hurt me to leave. One time I was in the bathtub, and she came in with a flaming oxtail pie." My skeptical response fazed him not at all. "It happened," he said. But the plan went awry.

"In becoming spoiled rotten, I became a little more human again," he said. "So a year later she told me what she had planned—and it was a delightful outcome." It was also an example of her accepting him, rather than acting on her feelings of being neglected. (To those who feel the oxtail pie incident is too much, I should add that on a number of occasions he has returned the act of generosity without the pie.)

Another example, more serious, is the story of a husband and wife with a troubled marriage, patients of psychiatrist Norman Paul, where the wife complained that for years her husband avoided kissing her, to the point of pressing his face into the pillow every time they made love. Only when Paul brought out the fact that from childhood the husband had hated the wet, smacking kisses of his mother did she understand it was not an act of rejection. That bit of perception came only after years of marriage, and my reaction upon reading it was, What a waste. Never to have asked? Never to have talked about it?

One of the really extraordinary pressures on the married couples I have talked with is that somehow they are expected, in our high-divorce society, to define *why* they remain together. No one is exactly standing at the bedroom door demanding, "What are your reasons for staying married?" But still, at different times they voiced the idea that to be married today is to feel faintly apologetic. It is a sign of a lack of imagination, as if one has not found oneself as a person. This is exactly the opposite of the way things were a few years ago: then, to be single was to be socially deficient. An amazing flip-flop.

It occurs to me that there is a major difference between the marriages of most middle-aged people today and those of their parents: this is the first generation with a very wide choice of partners. In times past, couples most likely would never have met unless they came from the same neighborhoods, went to the same schools, or were introduced by family friends. Marriage was not so much a matter of free choice as it was of proximity, and the reversal of that has profoundly influenced us, for good and ill. We choose our partners with less social constraint, but we lose the connecting links of shared religious or ethnic backgrounds, or simply the shared rhythms of life. Abie's Irish Rose may want to try out communal living, and what cultural shock waves does that set off?

The new twist on all this, the irony, is that to be married "by choice" now doesn't mean the freedom to choose one's spouse on the basis of one's own feelings. It means being free to choose not to be divorced, to resist jumping on the divorce bandwagon when things start getting rough, to ignore the popular assumption that a disposable culture is an efficient culture, that a troubled marriage can go out the door with last week's Handi-Wipes.

I'm not saying people discard their marriages with ease. That's a fiction. But divorce is so acceptable, so presumed. To choose not to be divorced (like any other freedom) brings its own uncertainty and anxiety. It is part of the flip-flop.

Another striking lesson of the marriages we've examined

is that almost any combination of two people can develop a working marriage, as long as the mix of caring and accommodating satisfies them—not anybody else. Vita Sackville-West and Harold Nicolson, with their homosexual affairs, practiced open marriage with a vengeance. Yet they stayed together, loved each other, and had a working marriage—based not on fidelity or compatibility but on that illusive "something else" that no one ever quite pins down, but which must be present. Everybody explains it differently. "We've been able to grow up together, as well as grow together," said Paul Newman, explaining why his marriage to Joanne Woodward has survived. "Aside from that, her interests are completely different from mine." Or Bianca Jagger, who ascribes her marital success with rock star Mick Jagger to the fact that they look alike. "I know people theorize Mick thought it would be amusing to marry his twin," she said. "But actually, he wanted to achieve the ultimate in loving himself." That suits her just fine.

Again, marriage is mystery and it is process. It changes and adapts, rises and falls. All change is inevitable, but when the mix is right, it doesn't bar long years of loving one person.

There it is—that sweeping word: love. Even to write it is to feel the need to neutralize it. It is the one four-letter word left that embarrasses or frightens. It carries a burden of multiple, conflicting meanings: honesty and hypocrisy; selfishness and unselfishness. It never quite means the same thing twice.

Recently I ran into a feminist friend who is very active in women's movement politics. I hadn't seen her in a couple of years and she told me she was about to be married. As we chatted about her plans to quit her job, start wallpapering, painting, sewing and cooking, I couldn't help marveling at her calm cheerfulness and nonapologetic manner.

"Jean," I asked, after we had laughed our way through the classic scene of admiring the engagement diamond, "what about your work in the feminist movement? What about the demonstrations and the organizing and all the other things you've done? Don't you believe in those things any more?"

"Oh yes, I do," she answered quickly. "But for me, those things aren't the most important things in life at this point. I believe life is modular. It's time now for me to move on to another module. I've spent eight years organizing and working for things I believe in, but now I want marriage. And children too, I hope." We smiled, wished each other well, and parted. I doubt if her name will cross my desk on a feminist press release again.

And that's okay, I thought later, really okay. Jean isn't letting anything or anybody down. She's simply moving on in the important business of living her life. I like her concept of life as modular very much. If we look back and try to touch the places where we were only a few years ago, many of us grope in empty space. So much has changed, so many people have gone away, so many new ones have appeared. We are rapidly becoming a nation of people not only unmoored but unstrung. So in our adapting American way, we pronounce the death of all that affirms continuity, because we can't make our connections with the past as we did before.

But the modular concept of life isn't necessarily the antithesis of continuity. It can instead put change into a more manageable perspective—because deal with change we must, whether we like it or not. That doesn't mean that we have to settle for aimless movement, forcing ourselves onto a track where the people we know, our jobs, the comforting routines of our lives, must pass by in a blur. Accepting change doesn't mean accepting internal emptiness. We can bid goodbye to what we cannot keep without feeling fear or betrayal, if we build each module on top of the one we inhabited before, taking with us those vital links we need with our own history for survival.

Only recently have psychologists and other researchers begun to pay attention to the developmental patterns of adults. For a society just barely hanging on through rapid change, it's about time. Men and women go through profound changes from the time they leave their families to marry and work, until the time they die. Marriages also go through similar cycles. Why do we persist in assuming the marriage embarked upon at the raw age of twenty will (read MUST) be the same at fifty? Why do we persist in assuming that marriages which do not stay the same will (read MUST) end in divorce?

What, finally, do these married couples value the most? What has been the prime thread of continuity through their marriages? It is a strong sense of shared history. They've lived with each other through bad times, good times, and forgettable times, and there isn't much of a way they can untangle the threads without losing basic parts of themselves. "How the hell would we divide everything up?" David said to Jan, and he wasn't talking only of the house and furniture.

They value this sense of shared history more than any

other single component. But there's much more needed to make a working marriage. History, at least a superficial variety, can consist of tracing a family's milestones in a photo album. They are aware of outside perils and are trying to build up inside strengths. They are imperfect, fragile, uncertain of each other at times. They are, in turn, depressed, angry, happy, sometimes content. Their marriages may stay strong, level out, or eventually fall apart, but what they are trying to do is accept each other, live together and be married.

These couples deal with the confinements of marriage by allowing individual freedom whatever way suits them best, and by rejecting outside definitions that suit them not at all. For most of them this attitude took time, trouble, and courage. But they have avoided the crippling confinement of marriage caused by living with the feeling of affection owed, and not freely given. Finally, when all is said and done, they consider themselves more whole within marriage than without, and they remain married for one essential reason—they want to be.

bibliography

Bergman, Ingmar. *Scenes from a Marriage: Six Dialogues for Television*. New York: Pantheon Books, 1974.

Bernard, Jesse. *The Future of Marriage*. New York: World Publishing Co., 1972.

Decter, Midge. *The Liberated Woman and Other Americans*. New York: Coward, McCann & Geoghegan, 1971.

DeMott, Benjamin. *Surviving the 70's*. New York: E. P. Dutton & Co., 1971.

Epstein, Joseph. *Divorced in America: Marriage in an Age of Possibility*. New York: E. P. Dutton & Co., 1974.

Howe, Louise Kapp, ed. *The Future of the Family*. New York: Simon and Schuster, 1972.

Janeway, Elizabeth. *Man's World, Woman's Place: A Study in Social Mythology*. New York: William Morrow and Co., 1971.

Lederer, William J., and Dr. Don D. Jackson. *The Mirages of Marriage*. New York: W. W. Norton & Co., 1968.

Lessing, Doris. *The Summer Before the Dark*. New York: Alfred A. Knopf, 1973.

Lurie, Alison. *The War Between the Tates*. New York: Random House, 1974.

MacPherson, Myra. *The Power Lovers: An Intimate Look at Politics and Marriage*. New York: G. P. Putnam's Sons, 1975.

May, Rollo. *Love and Will.* New York: W. W. Norton & Co., 1969.

O'Neill, Nena, and George O'Neill. *Shifting Gears.* New York: M. Evans and Company, 1974.

Parr, Jeanne. *The Superwives.* New York: Coward, McCann & Geoghegan, 1976.

Paul, Norman L., and Betty Byfield Paul. *A Marital Puzzle.* New York: W. W. Norton & Co., 1975.

Rogers, Carl R. *Becoming Partners: Marriage and Its Alternatives.* New York: Delacorte Press, 1972.

Russell, Bertrand. *Marriage and Morals.* New York: The Sun Dial Press, 1938.

Scanzoni, John. *Sexual Bargaining: Power Politics in the American Marriage.* Englewood Cliffs, N.J.: Prentice-Hall, 1972.

Shain, Merle. *Some Men Are More Perfect Than Others.* New York: Charterhouse Books, 1973.

Sheehy, Gail. *Passages: The Predictable Crises of Adult Life.* New York: E. P. Dutton & Co., 1976.

Weiss, Robert S. *Marital Separation.* New York: Basic Books, 1975.

Wolfe, Linda. *Playing Around: Women and Extra-Marital Sex.* New York: William Morrow and Co., 1974.

about the author

PATRICIA O'BRIEN is a columnist and Washington correspondent for the Detroit *Free Press*. She also hosts a public affairs television show in Chicago. A 1973 Nieman Fellow at Harvard University, she is the author of *The Woman Alone,* published in 1973.

Born in Somerville, Massachusetts, she lives with her four children in Chevy Chase, Maryland.